D0014572

EDWARD THOMAS

Matthew Hollis was born in Norwich in 1971. *Ground Water* (Bloodaxe, 2004) was shortlisted for the Guardian First Book Award, the Whitbread Prize for Poetry and the Forward Prize for Best First Collection. He is co-editor of *Strong Words: Modern Poets on Modern Poetry* (Bloodaxe, 2000) and *101 Poems Against War* (Faber, 2003), and editor of *Selected Poems of Edward Thomas* (Faber, 2011). *Now All Roads Lead to France: the Last Years of Edward Thomas* (Faber, 2011; Norton, 2012) won the Costa Biography Award and the H. W. Fisher Biography Prize and was Sunday Times Biography of the Year.

EDWARD THOMAS
Poems selected by MATTHEW HOLLIS

FABER & FABER

First published in 2011
by Faber & Faber Ltd
Bloomsbury House
74–77 Great Russell Street
London WC1B 3DA

This edition published in 2016

Printed in Great Britain by
CPI Group (UK) Ltd, Croydon, CR0 4YY

A CIP record for this book
is available from the British Library

ISBN 978-0-571-32877-2

10 9 8 7 6 5 4 3 2 1

Contents

Introduction

Perhaps no poet since Wordsworth walked as far as Edward Thomas. Some days he covered just a handful of miles in a loop of his cottage in the East Hampshire Hangers, other times he made fifteen or twenty-five miles in a day. For further distances he cycled, but he believed that the bicycle moved too quickly for him to pick out the kind of detail that would infuse his life's writing: the celandines on a grass verge, the honeysuckle in a hedgerow, the linnet in an elm tree.[1] He undertook these walks both alone and in company ('Tread as if you were walking in a dream,' he would tell a flagging companion) but always he walked through landscapes that would frame and fill his prose and his poems.[2]

'Almost as soon as I could babble I "babbled of green fields",' Thomas recalled, and yet for half his life he lived in the city, where his green fields were the commons of Wandsworth and Wimbledon or the holidays spent in Wiltshire and Wales.[3] He was born in south Lambeth in 1878 to a kindly but withdrawn mother and a stern, self-made civil-servant father who kept an eclectic library in the family home. His education was an assortment of board and private schools that his father pushed him through: among them, for a year and a term, St Paul's, until he failed to obtain a scholarship to cover his fees. But the school had at least developed in him what he called 'a faint ambition' to find work connected to literature, and through the father of the woman he would marry, Helen Noble, he continued a literary education that was always stirred by the outdoors more than it was by the classroom.[4] James Ashcroft Noble mentored the teenage Thomas in the writing of naturalist and topographic prose and helped him find publication when he was just nineteen: *The Woodland Life* (1897). When Thomas missed the first-class degree at Oxford that might have secured an academic career, it confirmed in his mind that it would be from freelance writing that he would earn his income.

As a literary critic he made barely more than an agricultural worker in his first year after university. He struggled to provide for his young family and took on ever more work, producing as many as one hundred reviews a year. He moved to the country – Kent at first and then Hampshire – and began to write books on commission, working hurriedly, exhaustedly and beneath his talents in a manner that would leave him feeling disgust at his literary output. But his income grew with his reputation as a critic and by 1906 was equivalent to a senior schoolmaster's, enough for the family to afford a housemaid. He was still in his twenties, but already he was probably the most fearless and influential of reviewers writing in the decade before the First World War, and did not hesitate to take his seniors to task wherever they fell short, be they Hardy, Bridges, Yeats or Kipling. He was also beginning to carve out a cogent style of topographical writing in *The Heart of England* (1906) and *The South Country* (1909), or in a study of the writer who had most influenced his own prose, *Richard Jefferies* (1909). The wildlife, the flora, the South Downs, the folk tales and country manners of his rural characters, and particularly the feeling for the plain rhythms of speech: these were all elements that emerged in his prose long before they found expression in verse.

Yet Thomas continued to make poor or financially motivated decisions about the literary work he would undertake that left him feeling defeated. His sense of self-worth was further diminished by a domestic situation that he frequently found suffocating and railed against, in so doing deepening the misery of his family and himself. His battle against depression was one he could not win; more than once he made preparations to take his own life. He sought medical insight for his affliction at a time when little was available, but in 1912 he came under the supervision of a bright young doctor called Godwin Baynes who pioneered an early form of psychoanalysis in England with Thomas as a trial patient. The clinical sessions had been going for a year when Thomas ended them abruptly; and though he was not cured of his condition, he had been encouraged in a method of self-inspection that would prove essential in his development as a writer.

It took Edward Thomas almost his lifetime to write poetry. When war broke out in the summer of 1914 he was thirty-six, a father of three, and had still not embarked upon his poems. He had written two dozen prose books and lent his name to a dozen more, but the unloosing of his verse needed a guide, a goader, a provocateur: that figure was Robert Frost. Four years Thomas's senior, Frost was thirty-nine when they met in 1913; he had published his debut book of poems in London only months before. Thomas identified the revolutionary power of the American's verse – and what he called his use of 'expressive intimate speech' – and praised his second book, *North of Boston*, to the skies.[5] Frost in turn recognised the latent poet languishing in Thomas, and encouraged him to revisit his prose and declare it in verse form in the very same cadence.

The poems came quickly to Edward Thomas, 'in a hurry and a whirl': more than 140 in barely two years. He revised very little, telling a friend that the poetry neither asked nor received much correction on paper.[6] Often he went back to his prose to find his poem. Sometimes his source was the notebook that he kept on his walks, other times his published prose. From the beginning, he established a method of evolved writing that he would carry into his verse: notebook entries, followed by interim prose, followed by final drafts. His field notes from 1 March 1896 were typical of the development of *The Woodland Life*, for example: 'Larks paired – fly hover & feed together,' which he then substantiated in a longhand diary: 'March 1. Larks have paired, and fly hover, and feed in couples; resorting often to the roadsides.' That entry was conflated with another which read, 'Larks, already banded, fly skipping across the clover, with but a chirrup of song,' and which in *The Woodland Life* finally became, 'Overhead, now and again, fly the banded larks bound for new feeding-grounds.'[7] When in 1914 it came to writing his first poems the method was initially the same, only this time the field notes became prose which then became verse. 'Up in the Wind' and 'Old Man' began with notebook jottings, followed by polished prose drafts, followed in turn by two verse drafts which led to a final poem for typing up. The length of time from notebook to typewriter could be a few days or many months, but the verse drafts that concluded the evolution were usually completed in a single day. Soon, he abandoned the interim prose altogether, but the notebooks remained a well to which he would return. Most of the first hundred or so poems that he wrote can be traced to such entries in his notes; others, such as 'Rain', were prised out of his existing prose publications, while many more shared phrases and thoughts with the letters he was writing at the time. This edition of his poetry includes a small selection of prose chosen to highlight Thomas's movement towards poetry.

'We were greater friends than almost any two ever were practising the same art,' said Frost; but the outbreak of war changed everything.[8] Frost returned to America and Thomas, against his initial judgement, went to war. 'A man enlists for some inexplicable reason which he may translate into simple, conventional terms,' Thomas wrote, but even so, his enlistment seemed particularly hard to fathom.[9] He was an anti-nationalist in a time before conscription, who loathed what he perceived to be the hypocrisy of the war, and despised the bigotry of the English newspapers more than he did any German opponent. These same papers had ceased to commission his kind of literary work since the outbreak of hostilities, leaving him without an income, and he considered following Frost to the States to farm, write or teach. But his deep attachment to the south country would swing his decision to enlist – a subtle, almost inexpressible desire to protect the soil, the scenery, the wildlife, and the ways of its people, a framework that had shaped his entire life and given him his livelihood; that, and a quarrel with Frost over his poem 'The Road Not Taken' at the very moment that emigration to America looked a certainty. The routine of army training alleviated some of the misery he experienced at home and afforded him time to write poems – fifty-nine of them as a soldier. For a year in 1915–16 he served with the Artists Rifles as a map-reading instructor in the comparative safety of an Essex training camp, but he transferred to the Royal Garrison Artillery as the lure of the front line grew ever stronger. Though he was a fine – and in his oblique approach to the conflict, a unique – war poet, he wrote no poems from the trenches.

Edward Thomas was a poet of strong gentleness, long in quick thinking. His poems rarely resolve; they avoid convenience, mistrust rhetoric and ostentation, and have the effect of lingering on the senses as a scent does or a thought on its way towards completion. He chose the phrase rather than the foot as his unit of composition, and would frequently break his rhythm inventively across his line-endings in ways that conjured the effect of a perpetually forming moment. He resisted the fashionable forms of the day, eschewed both the 'pomp' of the conservatives and the 'discord' of the modernisers, and put his trust in rhythms of speech at a time where this was not the received style.[10] His friend Walter de la Mare, for one, warned against the deployment of 'common speech' in poems, but Thomas would seek out the '"simple and direct" phrases' in all of his mature writing.[11] 'Only when a word has become necessary to him can a man use it safely,' he wrote in 1912, 'if he try to impress words by force on a sudden occasion, they will either perish by his violence or betray him' – simple enough advice for a poet of today, but counter to the often unnecessary and forced style of his peers at the time.[12]

In his craft Thomas learned much from Frost, but not in his philosophy, which was already fully formed and in print in the decade before the two men met. His verse lacked the surety and the irresistible cadence of his friend's, and his use of the line as a unit of sense was more circumspect than the American's; yet, at the same time, he achieved 'a tantalising vagueness' that Frost seldom risked but once said was the condition to which a poem should aspire.[13] It should be no surprise that Thomas, an assiduous critic, was a stern judge of his own achievements and considered himself, 'too ready to accept imitations'.[14] Certainly, there are moments when his early verse fell under the spell of Frost or resonated with lines from the poets he admired such as Hardy, de la Mare or W. H. Davies. But these occurrences are comparatively few and Frost was on good ground when he pronounced of Thomas, 'the accent is absolutely his own'.[15]

Twelve of Thomas's poems were published under the pseudonym 'Edward Eastaway' before he left for France in 1917; dozens more had been rejected by the literary magazines. But he lived just long enough to see his work showcased in an anthology of new poetry and even a favourable review that accompanied it. When *Poems* appeared in October 1917 he had been dead six months; a second volume, *Last Poems*, was issued the following year.

Through his walks, through his prose and through his verse, Edward Thomas brought an unrivalled eye to the English landscape at a moment where it was facing irreversible change. His attention to the natural world was never sentimental or proprietorial: he understood, as many of his peers seemed not to, that nature was in a state of constant flux and manipulation by man, and he knew, as a man, he could never enter the inner world of animals. But he instinctively understood the interdependence of humans and nature in a way that most of us require instruction on. In those terms, his work seems unfailingly modern, eerily attuned to our own ecological age, as relevant today as a century ago, or more so.

At twilight when walking, or at the parting of ways with a friend, he could feel great sadness that his journey must end; at times he determined that it should never cease.

Things will happen which will trample and pierce, but I shall go on, something that is here and there like the wind, something unconquerable, something not to be separated from the dark earth and the light sky, a strong citizen of infinity and eternity.[16]

He was killed on the first day of the Battle of Arras; he had survived little more than two months in France. Yet his personal war was never with a military opponent: it had been with his ravaging depression and with his struggle to find a literary expression through poetry that was worthy of his talents. And over the latter, at least, he won his battle.

NOTES

1. Edward Thomas, *In Pursuit of Spring*, London: Thomas Nelson, 1914, 199–200.
2. Eleanor Farjeon, *Edward Thomas: The Last Four Years*, London: Oxford University Press, 1958, 6.
3. Edward Thomas to H. N. Sturmer, 4 April 1900, Berg Collection, New York Public Library.
4. Edward Thomas, *Childhood of Edward Thomas: A Fragment of Autobiography*, London: Faber & Faber, 1938, 144.
5. Edward Thomas to Gordon Bottomley, 30 June 1915, Edward Thomas Collection, Cardiff University, *Letters to Gordon Bottomley* (ed. R. George Thomas), London: Oxford University Press, 1968, 251.
6. Edward Thomas to Gordon Bottomley, 30 June 1915, Cardiff, *Letters to Gordon Bottomley*, 250, 251.
7. Respectively: Field Notes, vol. 5, February–April 1896, Cardiff; 'A Diary in English Fields and Woods', 1 March 1896, in Edward Thomas, *The Woodland Life*, London: William Blackwood and Sons, 1897, 224; 'A Diary in English Fields and Woods', 16 July 1896, *The Woodland Life*, 187; and *The Woodland Life*, 113.

8. Robert Frost to Grace Walcott Conkling, 28 June 1921, *Poetry Wales*, vol. 13, no. 4 (Spring 1978), 22.

9. Edward Thomas, 'Tipperary', *The English Review*, October 1914, repr. in *The Last Sheaf*, London: Cape, 1928, 129.

10. Edward Thomas, 'A New Poet', *Daily News*, 22 July 1914.

11. Edward Thomas to Edward Garnett, *c*. mid-1909, Harry Ransom Center, University of Texas at Austin.

12. Edward Thomas, *Walter Pater: A Critical Study*, London: Martin Secker, 1913, 215.

13. Robert Frost to Louis Untermeyer, [1 Jan. 1916], *Selected Letters of Robert Frost* (ed. Lawrence Thompson), New York: Holt, Rinehart and Winston, 1964, 199.

14. Edward Thomas to Gordon Bottomley, 16 June 1915, Cardiff, *Letters to Gordon Bottomley*, 249.

15. Robert Frost to Grace Walcott Conkling, 28 June 1921, *Poetry Wales*, 22.

16. Edward Thomas, 'The Stile', *Light and Twilight*, London: Duckworth, 1911, 51.

Note on the Text

Edward Thomas's verse was published in two posthumous volumes by Selwyn and Blount: *Poems* in October 1917 and *Last Poems* in December 1918 (a small number of works were added to *Collected Poems* in 1920 and subsequent editions). Until 1981, it was thought that Thomas did not oversee the production of either volume, which accounts for the variant printings that appeared in editions up until that date (notably R. George Thomas's 1978 edition of the *Collected Poems*). But the emergence in 1981 of the printer's original typescript for *Poems*, now residing in the Bodleian Library, shows clearly that Thomas had prepared the collection himself: he had through-numbered it and marked a series of small emendations including titles to twenty-three poems added by hand. With the exception of setting errors introduced by the printer, the text of *Poems* (and its titles) can be considered reliable from an authorial point of view, even though Thomas never saw the proofs (he had asked his friends Eleanor Farjeon and John Freeman to supervise the book through the press while he was in France). The same friends appear to have assembled *Last Poems* in its entirety from typescripts that were in circulation. Unlike *Poems*, the ordering, the selection of drafts and (in some places) the giving of titles in *Last Poems* was made not by Thomas but most likely by Farjeon and Freeman; for this reason, we cannot be certain that the published text reflected Thomas's final wishes.

In making the selection for this volume, I have followed the text of *Poems* (correcting printer's errors) and have treated contributions from *Last Poems* on a case-by-case basis, returning to the original manuscripts and typescripts in an attempt to discern Thomas's intentions. Text sources and initial publication details are provided in the section of notes that follows the poems; where titles are not Thomas's own, these too are given in the notes.

In transcribing the notebooks, I have retained Thomas's original abbreviations, but have expanded them in square brackets on first appearance and subsequently as necessary; round brackets are the author's markings.

*

I am grateful to the Estate of Edward Thomas, to Cardiff University Library: Special Collections and to the Poetry Collection of the University Libraries, University at Buffalo, The State University of New York.

Table of Dates

1908		more than 130 reviews
1909	Jan.	*Richard Jefferies* (Hutchinson)
	Nov.	*The South Country* (J. M. Dent)
	Dec.	Wick Green, Froxfield, Steep, Hampshire
		more than 110 reviews
1910		*Rest and Unrest* (Duckworth)
		Rose Acre Papers, revised edition (Duckworth)
	June	*Windsor Castle* (Blackie and Son)
	Aug.	*b.* Myfanwy Thomas (daughter)
	Nov.	*Feminine Influence on the Poets* (Martin Secker)
		14 articles and more than 130 reviews
1911		*Light and Twilight* (Duckworth)
		Celtic Stories (Clarendon Press)
	Sep.	severe nervous breakdown
	Oct.	*Maurice Maeterlinck* (Methuen)
	Nov.	*The Tenth Muse* (Martin Secker)
	Dec.	*The Isle of Wight* (Blackie and Son)
1912	*c.* Jan.	*George Borrow* (Chapman & Hall)
	Jul.	*Norse Tales* (Clarendon Press)
	Sep.	*Lafcadio Hearn* (Constable)
	Nov.	*Algernon Charles Swinburne: A Critical Study*
		(Martin Secker)
1913	Mar.	*The Icknield Way* (Constable)
	c. July	*The Country* (B. T. Batsford)
	July	2 Yew Tree Cottage, Steep, Hampshire
	Oct.	*Walter Pater: A Critical Study* (Martin Secker)
	Oct.	meets Robert Frost
	Nov.	*The Happy-Go-Lucky Morgans* (Duckworth)
1914	Apr.	*In Pursuit of Spring* (Thomas Nelson and Sons)
	July	reviews Robert Frost's *North of Boston*
	Aug.	World War I begins
	Dec.	completes 'Up in the Wind' (first poem)
1915	Feb.	Frost returns to America
	June	receives 'The Road Not Taken' from Frost
	July	enlists in the Artists Rifles

1915	Sep.	High Beech Camp, Loughton, Essex
	Oct.	*Four-and-Twenty Blackbirds* (Duckworth)
	Oct.	*The Life of the Duke of Marlborough* (Chapman & Hall)
	Oct.	*This England*, editor (Oxford University Press)
	Nov.	Hare Hall Camp, Gidea Park, Essex
1916		*Six Poems* (Pear Tree Press)
	Aug.	enlists in the Royal Artillery
	Sep.	Royal Artillery Barracks, Trowbridge, Wiltshire
	Dec.	244 Siege Battery, Royal Garrison Artillery, Lydd, Kent
	Dec.	completes *Poems*
	Dec.	*Keats* (T. C. & E. C. Jack)
1917	Jan.	embarks for France
	Feb.	'Old Man' published in *Poetry* (Chicago)
	Mar.	*An Anthology of New Poetry*, contributor (Constable)
	Apr.	*d*. in Arras, France
	Apr.	'Adlestrop' published in *New Statesman*
	Sep.	*A Literary Pilgrim in England* (Methuen)
	Oct.	*Poems* (Selwyn and Blount)
1918	Nov.	World War I ends
	Dec.	*Last Poems* (Selwyn and Blount)
1920	Sep.	*Collected Poems* (Selwyn and Blount)

This is the constellation of the Lyre:
Its music cannot ever tire,
For it is silent. No man need fear it:
Unless he wants to, he will not hear it.

E. J.

EDWARD THOMAS

A Diary in English Fields and Woods

Between the spring of 1895 and 1896, Thomas kept a diary from his visits to Richmond Park, Wiltshire and Surrey that he intended to use to inform the essays he was writing for his first book, *The Woodland Life*, published in 1897. The book itself was filled with heavy, overwrought prose, but the original diary entries (included at the end of the book at the suggestion of Thomas's mentor, James Ashford Noble) foretold the direction in tone and content that his poems would take twenty years later.

April 12 Cuckoo at Wimbledon crying in the oaks; and below him the first wood-anemones, flushed white. Young rooks and thrushes in the nest.

May 2 Orange-tip butterflies first seen, threading the coppice with a flight like blown leaves.

Early field scorpion-grass, a miniature hairy forget-me-not, blossoming from crannies in an old ha-ha: pale blue, earliest of its kind.

Mares'-tails not only grow in marshy land and even quite submerged, but in the driest spots, such as seldom-used railway embankments where the riddled chalk will not hold water an hour: here it grows, among the metals, with colts-foot and wild carrot and poppy.

June 5 The first wild rose of the summer.

Several nightingales have ceased to sing.

At one time sand-martins built at the very edge of Swindon old town in 'the Quarries'; but frequent blastings and the invasion of starlings and sparrows have exiled them.

July 5 Last cry of the cuckoo.

Yellow-ammer yet sings.

Sparrows flocking in the unmown fields: as they rise their combined wings sound like a horse shaking himself in the meads.

Peewits flocking: in much the same numbers as will be seen henceforward until March.

August 5 Swifts abound in Richmond Park, haunting the ponds there with the swallows and martins.

This wet weather succeeding the late drought favours the pheasant-rearing.

Crows do far more harm to the game in the Park than hawks: the former use art, and sidle up and wait about all day; the latter dash, gain or miss, and are off. But a hawk will on occasion seize a chick, or more often the nestling of a song-bird, under the very mouth of the gun.

The arrival of a hawk is rare and noteworthy now, and though a pair will haunt the plantations with the intent of breeding, it is very rarely that they succeed even in building a nest – far more seldom do they hatch. They, with the jays (so common near by, at Wimbledon) and rarer magpies, are ruthlessly shot.

Stoats and weasels are trapped and shot; and, so ill has this exterminating work been carried out, not one has been seen this summer.

Owls visit and are shot here.

Peewits once haunted the low greensward, rush-tufted, that sweeps to the larger ponds.

7.30 p.m. the herons return to their nesting trees: five of the birds in close company came over from the west. Each wing-stroke lifts the bird perceptibly, but its course is not thus altered, sinking as it does in the distinct interval between each flap.

September 9 Swallows and martins still at their nests, where the weak young chirrup.

Sycamore foliage darkening, but unflushed.

Bats fly in the evenings: and even in treeless London streets, where lodging for them seems wanting.

Air suddenly thick with elm-leaves falling: on the sward the decay is beautiful until the rains and winds have huddled them, stained and warped, into the root-hollows of the trees.

The winds become more keen in the thinning trees; and autumn is in the air despite an opulence of sunlight.

October 3 Harebells flowering, and throughout the month, with dwarf red-rattle, among the rush-tufts with lipped flowers and mossy thick leaves; sheep's scabious; ragwort; hawkweeds; field speedwell; yarrow; second woodbine wreaths; tormentil; buttercup; bramble; dove's-foot crane's-bill; herb Robert; wild thyme; eye-bright; black knapweed; and wild parsnip.

November 8 After heavy rain the elms are stained down their grey bark as if seared with heated iron; beeches also are marked black down their green-coated boles by spring-like rills of rain from above, or by condensed mist.

Fog pierces where rain and wind cannot, and is more terrible than all to the wild things of the wood – more certain even than frost.

Two elms in a Croydon hollow, purely green and unchanged apparently by autumn; but elsewhere the elms are leafless. It is noticeable that leaves in bunches still cling to elms and poplars in London streets, where the trees are neighboured by gas-lamps. The heat, though intermittent, appears to be the cause of this.

December 7 Snow lightly around, yet I see spring signs: delicate new sprouts of many herbs – ground-ivy, goose-grass, nettle, wild parsnip – all pale with youth; sticky young shoots about the flaky yew-bole.

January 7 Year opens mild, with the happy songs of black-bird and thrush thick in the woods; green shoots rising everywhere; all life is quick and glad; the fallow deer idle in the tempered sun under the oaks at Richmond, or sip the water through budding buttercups and weeds.

Wood-pigeons crowd to the oaks at sundown, clattering loudly.

February 26 The hare in his form rises slowly bit by bit, and returns, as carefully, after a stretch of his hind-legs or reconnoitre.

March 28 Orchard trees lit with blossom.

Chestnuts coming into leaf.

The Woodland Life, 162–233

Llewelyn, the Bard

In 1905, Thomas published a 'translation' in *Beautiful Wales* under the guise of a fictitious poet, Llewelyn, the Bard. When he admitted that the work was in fact his own, a friend encouraged him to write more verse, but Thomas replied, 'I do not know how to do the trick again' (to Gordon Bottomley, 30 June 1905). It would take almost a decade for Thomas to recover the 'trick', although he would have another near encounter, which he recorded in 'Insomnia' (27).

And here is one of his [the Bard's] imitative songs, reduced to its lowest terms by a translator:

She is dead, Eluned,
Whom the young men and the old men
And the old women and even the young women
Came to the gates in the village
To see, because she walked as beautifully as a heifer.

She is dead, Eluned,
Who sang the new songs
And the old; and made the new
Seem old, and the old
As if they were just born and she had christened them.

She is dead, Eluned,
Whom I admired and loved,
When she was gathering red apples,
When she was making bread and cakes,
When she was smiling to herself and not thinking of me.

[7]

She is dead, Eluned,
Who was part of Spring,
And of blue Summer and red Autumn,
And made the Winter beloved;
She is dead, and these things come not again.

Beautiful Wales, 82–3

[Love Poetry]

Thomas frequently wrote autobiography into his prose, sometimes deploying fictive or allegorical characters to mask his appearance, other times barely attempting to conceal the representation of himself. But in *Feminine Influence on the Poets* (1910), he declared a distance between the circumstances of an author's life and the subject matter of their work, and chose the most intimate subject of all to make his point: love poetry.

Love opens the door, but it does not know what is within, whether it be treasure, nothingness or devils; and of the unimagined things beyond the door love-poetry is the revelation. That love-poetry seems so often to have little to do with love is because we forget that there are matters in the presence of which any man and Shakespeare are equally impotent and silent. Many love-poems were never shown to their begetters, many would not have moved them nor were in a sense meant for them at all. The love-poem is not for the beloved, for it is not worthy, as it is the least thing that is given to her, and none knows this better than she unless it be the lover. It is written in solitude, is spent in silence and the night like a sigh with an unknown object. It may open with desire of woman, but it ends with unexpected consolation or with another desire not of woman. Love-poetry, like all other lyric poetry, is in a sense unintentionally overheard, and only by accident and in part understood, since it is written not for any one, far less for the public, but for the understanding spirit that is in the air round about or in the sky or somewhere.

It is not only the present or past lover of one particular woman that can read and penetrate and enjoy love-poems, and this fact alone might show how vain it is to regard them as addressed merely to those whose names they may bear. When do the words of love-poems come into the mind or on to the lips? It is upon a hundred different occasions having nothing in common save that beauty is there or is desired. The sight of a fine landscape, recovery from sickness, rain in spring, music of bird or instrument or human voice, may at any time evoke as the utterance of our hearts the words long ago addressed to a woman who never saw them, and is now dead. And as these things revive poems in the mind of a reader, so certainly they have given birth to some of those poems in the minds of poets; and the figure of a woman is introduced unwittingly as a symbol of they know not what, perhaps only of desire; or if there is no woman mentioned, it will as often as not bring one into the thoughts and so prove, if need were, that hers was the original incantation. We treat them as parts written for ourselves to act, in the spirit, as they were written by the poet, in the spirit.

Feminine Influence on the Poets, 76–7

[Words and Subject Matter]

Through poetry, Thomas strove to adopt a language that was neither literary nor ornamental but drawn from the common speech, 'a language not be to betrayed' ('I never saw that land before'). In his 1911 biography of the writer Maurice Maeterlinck (1862–1949), he espouses a vocabulary and subject matter that are commonplace rather than poetic, as well as a belief that a poem must be a self-sustaining entity, not dependent on references outside of it.

[N]o word, outside works of information, has any value beyond its surface value except what it receives from its neighbours and its position among them. Each man makes his own language in the main unconsciously and inexplicably, unless he is still at an age when he is an admiring but purely aesthetic collector of words; certain words – he knows not why – he will never use; and there are a hundred peculiarities in his rhythms and groupings to be discovered. In the mainly instinctive use of his language the words will all support one another, and, if the writing is good, the result of this support is that each word is living its intensest life. The first few words of a work of art teach us, though we do not know it at the time, exactly how much value we are to give to all the rest, whether they are to be words only, or images, or spirits. They admit us, or teach us that we cannot be admitted, to the author's world. Any writer whose words have this power may make a poem of anything – a story, a dream, a thought, a picture, an ejaculation, a conversation. Whatever be the subject, the poem must not depend for its main effect upon anything outside itself except the humanity of the reader. It may please for the moment by the aid of some irrelevant and transitory interest – political interest, for example; but, sooner or later, it will be left naked and solitary, and will so be judged, and if it does not create about itself a world of its own it is condemned to endure the death which is its element. These worlds of living poems may be of many different kinds. As a rule they are regions of the earth now for the first time separated from the rest and made independent; they may be lit by the sun of every one, or by another, or by the moon, or by a green lantern: whatever they are, they are stronger than this world, and their light more steadfast than sun or moon. Wordsworth writes a poem in the hope of making it give the same impression as a certain hawthorn-tree gives to him; Keats because he cannot dismiss from his mind the words, 'Dost thou not hear the sea?'; Burns because a girl pleases and evades him Anything, however small, may make a poem; nothing, however great, is certain to.

Maurice Maeterlinck, 27–8

How I Began

'How I Began' was the first of the openly autobiographical prose pieces that Thomas published while undergoing psychotherapy in 1913. Here, in recording his earliest interest in writing, he outlines the method of keeping notebooks that would inform both his prose and his poetry.

Talking prose is natural to most of the species; writing it is now almost as common, if not as natural; having it published when written is the third step which distinguishes an author from the more primitive minority of mankind. No author, I suppose, except Miss Helen Keller, has varied this method of progress. Every one begins by talking, stumbles into writing, and succumbs to print.

The first step is the most interesting and the most difficult to explain and describe. I shall leave it alone. The second step is very interesting, and less difficult to explain and describe, yet I can remember little of it. I can only remark here that the result of teaching a child to read before it can write is that it begins and usually ends by writing like a book, not like a human being. It was my own experience. From the age of one, I could express by words and inflections of the voice all that ever sought expression within me, from feelings of heat, cold, hunger, repletion, indigestion, etc., to subtle preferences of persons and things. But when I came to write the slowness of that unnatural act decimated and disconcerted my natural faculties. I laboriously covered a square foot of notepaper, communicating nothing much beyond the fact that I had begun to hold a pen, and to master English grammar.

That the best of fountain-pens is slow, does not entirely account for the inexpressiveness of that square foot of notepaper. The slowness made it practically impossible to say what I was thinking, even if I had tried. I did not try hard. I do not believe that it was by any means my sole or chief aim to write what I was thinking, or what I should have spoken had my correspondent been in the same room with me. I felt it to be highly important that I should use terms such as I had met in books, seldom if ever in speech. Nor do I remember hearing it said that I could, or should, write as I thought or as I spoke.

Until the age of eight or nine, therefore, all my writing was painful and compulsory, and I knew well that it displayed a poorer creature than the severest critic could judge me. But at that age I was given a small notebook in a cover as much like tortoiseshell as could be made for a penny. In this I wrote down a number of observations of my own accord, though I dare say the notebook had been designed as a trap; if there was a separate bait, I have forgotten it. All that I can remember is that I pronounced the houses of Swindon to be 'like bull-dogs, small but strongly built'. They were of stone, and I was accustomed to brick. Stone seemed to be a grander material. Hence the note. The sententious form was, no doubt, due to a conscious desire to be impressive, that is to say, adult. It was not the last time I experienced this desire, but I shall not trouble you with more instances.

With short intervals, from that time onwards I was a writer by choice. I began several diaries, carrying on the entries in some of them as far as February. By the time I was fourteen or fifteen, I did more; I kept a more or less daily record of notable events, the finding of birds' nests, the catching of moles or fish, the skinning of a stoat, the reading of Richard Jefferies and the naturalists.

These notes aimed at brevity: they were above syntax and indifferent to dignity. I was not, however, permitted to forget syntax or dignity. I was obliged to write essays on Imperial Federation, the Greek Colonization of Sicily, Holidays, etc., where I gave myself up to an almost purely artistic rendering of such facts as I remembered, and such opinions as I could concoct by the help of memory, fancy, and the radical and the free-thinking influence of home. Thus, like nearly every other child, I virtually neglected in my writing the feelings that belonged to my own nature and my own times of life – an irreparable loss, whether great or not. If I wrote about what really pleased or concerned me, like a walk all day or all night in Wiltshire, I had in view not the truth but the eyes of elders, and those elders clothed in the excess and circumstance of elderliness regularly assumed in the presence of children. I was considered to excel in this form of rhetoric. So seriously, too, did I take myself in it, that from the time I was sixteen I found myself hardly letting a week pass without writing one or two descriptions – of a man, or a place, or a walk – in a manner largely founded on Jefferies' *Amateur Poacher*, Kingsley's *Prose Idylls*, and Mr Francis A. Knight's weekly contributions to the *Daily News*, but doubtless with tones supplied also by Shelley and Keats, and later on by Ruskin, De Quincey, Pater, and Sir Thomas Browne. I had quite a number of temptations to print, and at the age of fifteen easily gave way. At seventeen, some of those descriptions were printed in the *Speaker* and the *New Age*, and soon afterwards took the form of a book.

While I was afflicted with serious English compos-ition and English literature, I was reading Scott, Fenimore Cooper, Henty, and the travellers, because I loved them;

I was also thinking and talking in a manner which owed little to those dignified exercises, though the day was to come when I spoke very much as I wrote. Presently, also, myself and English, as she is taught in schools, came to a conflict, and gradually to a more and more friendly agreement through the necessity of writing long letters daily to one who was neither a schoolboy nor an elder, the subject of the letters being matters concerning nobody else in the world. Now it was that I had a chance of discarding or of adapting to my own purpose the fine words and infinite variety of constructions which I had formerly admired from afar off and imitated in fairly cold blood. There is no doubt that my masters often lent me dignity and subtlety altogether beyond my needs.

Both in these letters and in papers intended for print, I ravaged the language (to the best of my ability) at least as much for ostentation as for use, though I should not like to have to separate the two. This must always happen where a man has collected all the colours of the rainbow, 'of earthquake and eclipse', on his palette, and has a cottage or a gasometer to paint. A continual negotiation was going on between thought, speech and writing, thought having as a rule the worst of it. Speech was humble and creeping, but wanted too many fine shades and could never come to a satisfactory end. Writing was lordly and regardless. Thought went on in the twilight, and wished the other two might come to terms for ever. But maybe they did not and never will, and, perhaps, they never do. In my own case, at any rate, I cannot pronounce, though I have by this time provided an abundance of material for a judgment.

T.P.'s Weekly, 31 January 1913, repr. in *The Last Sheaf*, 15–20

[Rain]

The Icknield Way, Thomas's homage to the ancient road
from East Anglia to the West Country, was written in 1911
and published in 1913. Thomas's depression was acute at
the time of his journey, and on one evening of downpour in
Berkshire it threatened to overwhelm him in a passage
which he later drew upon in composing his poem 'Rain'
(110) in 1916.

I lay awake listening to the rain, and at first it was as pleas-
ant to my ear and my mind as it had long been desired; but
before I fell asleep it had become a majestic and finally a
terrible thing, instead of a sweet sound and symbol. It was
accusing and trying me and passing judgment. Long I lay
still under the sentence, listening to the rain, and then
at last listening to words which seemed to be spoken by
a ghostly double beside me. He was muttering: The all-
night rain puts out summer like a torch. In the heavy, black
rain falling straight from invisible, dark sky to invisible,
dark earth the heat of summer is annihilated, the splendour
is dead, the summer is gone. The midnight rain buries it
away where it has buried all sound but its own. I am alone
in the dark still night, and my ear listens to the rain piping
in the gutters and roaring softly in the trees of the world.
Even so will the rain fall darkly upon the grass over the
grave when my ears can hear it no more. I have been glad
of the sound of rain, and wildly sad of it in the past; but that
is all over as if it had never been; my eye is dull and my
heart beating evenly and quietly; I stir neither foot nor
hand; I shall not be quieter when I lie under the wet grass

and the rain falls, and I of less account than the grass. The summer is gone, and never can it return. There will never be any summer any more, and I am weary of everything. I stay because I am too weak to go. I crawl on because it is easier than to stop. I put my face to the window. There is nothing out there but the blackness and sound of rain. Neither when I shut my eyes can I see anything. I am alone. Once I heard through the rain a bird's questioning watery cry – once only and suddenly. It seemed content, and the solitary note brought up against me the order of nature, all its beauty, exuberance, and everlastingness like an accusation. I am not a part of nature. I am alone. There is nothing else in my world but my dead heart and brain within me and the rain without. Once there was summer, and a great heat and splendour over the earth terrified me and asked me what I could show that was worthy of such an earth. It smote and humiliated me, yet I had eyes to behold it, and I prostrated myself, and by adoration made myself worthy of the splendour. Was I not once blind to the splendour because there was something within me equal to itself? What was it? Love . . . a name! . . . a word! . . . less than the watery question of the bird out in the rain. The rain has drowned the splendour. Everything is drowned and dead, all that was once lovely and alive in the world, all that had once been alive and was memorable though dead is now dung for a future that is infinitely less than the falling dark rain. For a moment the mind's eye and ear pretend to see and hear what theeye and ear themselves once knew with delight. The rain denies. There is nothing to be seen or heard, and there never was. Memory, the last chord of the lute, is broken. The rain has been and will be for ever over the earth. There never was anything but the dark rain.

Beauty and strength are as nothing to it. Eyes could not flash in it.

I have been lying dreaming until now, and now I have awakened, and there is still nothing but the rain. I am alone. The unborn is not more weak or more ignorant, and like the unborn I wait and wait, knowing neither what has been nor what is to come, because of the rain, which is, has been, and must be. The house is still and silent, and those small noises that make me start are only the imagination of the spirit or they are the rain. There is only the rain for it to feed on and to crawl in. The rain swallows it up as the sea does its own foam. I will lie still and stretch out my body and close my eyes. My breath is all that has been spared by the rain, and that comes softly and at long intervals, as if it were trying to hide itself from the rain. I feel that I am so little I have crept away into a corner and been forgotten by the rain. All else has perished except me and the rain. There is no room for anything in the world but the rain. It alone is great and strong. It alone knows joy. It chants monotonous praise of the order of nature, which I have disobeyed or slipped out of. I have done evilly and weakly, and I have left undone. Fool! you never were alive. Lie still. Stretch out yourself like foam on a wave, and think no more of good or evil. There was no good and no evil. There was life and there was death, and you chose. Now there is neither life nor death, but only the rain. Sleep as all things, past, present, and future, lie still and sleep, except the rain, the heavy, black rain falling straight through the air that was once a sea of life. That was a dream only. The truth is that the rain falls for ever and I am melting into it. Black and monotonously sounding is the midnight and solitude of the rain. In a little while or in an age – for it is all one – I shall know the full truth of the words I used to love, I knew not why, in my days of nature, in the days before the rain: 'Blessed are the dead that the rain rains on.'

The Icknield Way, 280–3

[On Style]

Edward Thomas was once an admirer of the prose style of
Walter Pater (1839–94), but in writing his biography, pub-
lished in 1913, Thomas came to believe that Pater's work
contained a fundamental flaw: the absence of an expressive
rhythm drawn from speech patterns and delivered via the
ear. Written in 1911–12, and published before he had met
Robert Frost, Thomas's commentary on Pater shows his
own contribution to the ideas that he would share with
Frost about 'the sound of sense'.

The most and the greatest of man's powers are as yet little
known to him, and are scarcely more under his control
than the weather: he cannot keep a shop without trusting
somewhat to his unknown powers, nor can he write books
except such as are no books. It appears to have been Pater's
chief fault, or the cause of his faults, that he trusted those
powers too little. The alternative supposition is that he did
not carry his self-conscious labours far enough. On almost
every page of his writing words are to be seen sticking out,
like the raisins that will get burnt on an ill-made cake. It is
clear that they have been carefully chosen as the right and
effective words, but they stick out because the labour of
composition has become so self-conscious and mechanical
that cohesion and perfect consistency are impossible. The
words have only an isolated value; they are labels; they
are shorthand: they are anything but living and social
words. [. . .]

Pater was, in fact, forced against his judgment to use
words as bricks, as tin soldiers, instead of flesh and blood

and genius. Inability to survey the whole history of every word must force the perfectly self-conscious writer into this position. Only when a word has become necessary to him can a man use it safely; if he try to impress words by force on a sudden occasion, they will either perish of his violence or betray him. No man can decree the value of one word, unless it is his own invention; the value which it will have in his hands has been decreed by his own past, by the past of his race. It is, of course, impossible to study words too deeply, though all men are not born for this study: but Pater's influence has tended to encourage meticulosity in detail and single words, rather than a regard for form in its largest sense. His words and still less his disciples' have not been lived with sufficiently. Unless a man write with his whole nature concentrated upon his subject he is unlikely to take hold of another man. For that man will read, not as a scholar, a philologist, a word-fancier, but as a man with all his race, age, class, and personal experience brought to bear on the matter. [. . .]

When words are used like bricks they are likely to inflict yet another punishment on the abuser, so making it more than ever impossible that they will justly represent 'the conscious motions of a convinced intelligible soul'. They refuse to fall into the rhythms which only emotion can command. The rhythms satisfactory to the mere naked ear are of little value: they will be so much sonority or suavity. How rhythm is commonly regarded may be shown by the following: –

The sentence can have two other qualities, rhythm and a certain cadence, light or grave, or of some other kind, in harmony with its meaning. These graces of the sentence are best regarded as refinements added to its essential and indispensable qualities.

Here again appears the necessity for the aid of speech in literature. Nothing so much as the writer's rhythm can give that intimate effect 'as if he had been talking'. Rhythm is of the essence of a sincere expressive style. [. . .]

It is, of course, true that writing stands for thought, not speech, and there is a music of words which is beyond speech; it is an enduring echo of we know not what in the past and in the abyss, an echo heard in poetry and the utterance of children; and prose, if 'born of conversation', is 'enlivened and invigorated by poetry'. But is it true there is a harmony which the ear cannot acknowledge? Has not the eye the power to act as a ghostly messenger to the ear? I doubt whether Pater's sidelong, pausing sentences have any kind of value as harmony, heard or unheard. It might be retorted, in the words of Joubert, that 'he who never thinks beyond what he says, nor sees beyond what he thinks, has a downright style', that there is 'a vulgar naturalness, and an exquisite naturalness', and no one would expect of Pater a downright style or a vulgar naturalness. It may be retorted again that Pepys is often intimate without aid of rhythm. But a diary, more or less in shorthand, is no argument. And if it is a question of naturalness, even an exquisite naturalness is hard to attain, when the writing, disturbed by protuberant words, has no continuous rhythm to give it movement and coherence. What Pater has attained is an exquisite unnaturalness.

Walter Pater, 213–20

[The Other Man]

In March 1913, Thomas spent a week cycling from London to Somerset in an attempt to track the arrival of spring. *In Pursuit of Spring* was published in 1914 and was the book that Robert Frost highlighted when he urged Thomas to recast his prose in verse form using the exactly the same cadence. The figure of the 'other', an alter ego that symbolised what Thomas once called his 'joint tenancy', had appeared in his prose already; but with *In Pursuit of Spring* the doppelgänger took its most forceful form yet, and would inform Thomas's 1914 poem 'The Other' (55).

As I sat there, who should come up and stare at the chapel on the bridge and its weather-vane of a gilded perch, but the Other Man. Surprise sufficiently fortified whatever pleasure we felt to compel us to join company; for he also was going to Wells.

We took the Frome road as far as Winkfield, where we turned off westward to Farleigh Hungerford. In half a mile we were in Somerset, descending by a steep bank of celandines under beeches that rose up on our right towards the Frome. The river lay clear ahead of us, and to our left. A bushy hill, terraced horizontally, rose beyond it, and Farleigh Hungerford Castle, an ivied front, a hollow-eyed round tower, and a gateway, faced us from the brow. From the bridge, and the ruined cottages and mills collected round it, we walked up to the castle, which is a show place. From here the Other Man would have me turn aside to see Tellisford. This is a hamlet scattered along half a mile of by-road, from a church at the corner down to the Frome.

Once there was a ford, but now you cross by a stone footbridge with white wooden handrails. A ruined flock-mill and a ruined ancient house stand next to it on one side; on the other the only house is a farm with a round tower embodied in its front. Away from this farm a beautiful meadow slopes between the river and the woods above. This grass, which becomes level for a few yards nearest the bank, was the best possible place, said the Other Man, for running in the sun after bathing at the weir – we could see its white wall of foam half a mile higher up the river, which was concealed by alders beyond. He said it was a great haunt of nightingales. And there was also a service tree; and, said he, in that tree sang a thrush all through May – it was the best May that ever was – and so well it sang, unlike any other thrush, that it made him think he would gladly live no longer than a thrush if he could do some one thing as right, as crisp and rich, as the song was. 'I suppose you write books,' said I. 'I do,' said he. 'What sort of books do you write?' 'I wrote one all about this valley of the Frome. . . . But no one knows that it was the Frome I meant. You look surprised. Nevertheless, I got fifty pounds for it.' 'That is a lot of money for such a book!' 'So my publisher thought.' 'And you are lucky to get money for doing what you like.' 'What I like!' he muttered, pushing his bicycle back uphill, past the goats by the ruin, and up the steps between walls that were lovely with humid moneywort, and saxifrage like filigree, and ivy-leaved toadflax. Apparently the effort loosened his tongue. He rambled on and on about himself, his past, his writing, his digestion; his main point being that he did not like writing. He had been attempting the impossible task of reducing undigested notes about all sorts of details to a grammatical, continuous narrative. He abused notebooks violently. He said that they blinded him to nearly everything that would not go into the form of notes; or, at any rate, he could never afterwards reproduce the great effects of Nature and fill in the interstices merely – which was all they were good for – from the notes. The notes – often of things which he would otherwise have forgotten – had to fill the whole canvas. Whereas, if he had taken none, then only the important, what he truly cared for, would have survived in his memory, arranged not perhaps as they were in Nature, but at least according to the tendencies of his own spirit. 'Good God!' said he. But luckily we were by this time on the level. I mounted. He followed.

In Pursuit of Spring, 217–20

Insomnia

On 6 September 1913, Edward Thomas stayed at the home of Vivian Locke Ellis in East Grinstead. During a night of troubled sleep, lines of poetry came to him which he attempted to remember by casting into verse 'and failing very badly indeed', he wrote to Walter de la Mare the following day (Bodleian Library). Though he was still more than a year away from completing his first mature poem, 'Insomnia', written in the autumn of 1913, showed Thomas encountering the possibility that he might after all become a poet.

Night after night deliberately we take upon ourselves the utmost possible weakness, because it is the offering most acceptable to sleep. Our thick coverings give us warmth without need of motion. The night air we moderate into a harmless rustling or stroking coolness; or, if it be an obstreperous air, we may shut it out altogether, and with it all sounds. We choose to be alone, and in darkness. We make ourselves so weak, so easy, so content with nothing, that scarce anything but personal danger, and that immediate and certain, could stir us. Thus cunningly we oppose the utmost possible weakness to the assault of sleep.

Sometimes I have a lighted candle and a book at my bedside, but seldom for more than five minutes. The light and the effort of reading, though I may have gone early to bed, are too much for my instinctive weakness, this religious malingering. I find that I desire to enter without gradation into perfect helplessness, and I exercise a quiet resolution against the strains even of memory. For once I have lain down, safe, warm, and unanxious, nothing I can remember is worthy for more than a moment to interrupt. In this weakness there is a kind of power. Still and relaxed, as it were lacking bones and muscles entirely, I lie in a composed eagerness for sleep. And most often sleep will stoop and swallow me up, and I have no more dream or trouble than a grain swallowed by a bird.

But the mighty weakness that so allures sleep is turned to a powerless strength during the night. I wake before dawn, and then, much as I desire sleep, I cannot have it. I am now the prey of anything but sleep, anything real or unreal that comes to sight, touch, or hearing, or straight to the brain. It seems that all night I have heard the poplars shivering across the street in the strong lamplight, with a high singing note like a flame instead of a noise of showers; it seems that this shivering and this light will continue for ever, and for ever shall I lie restless under their afflictions. I strive, but no longer with unconscious power, to sink into the weakness that commands or deserves sleep. Any memory now can discompose me; any face, any word, any event, out of the past has to be entertained for a minute or an hour, according to its will, not mine. Those poplar leaves in the bright street are mightier than I or sleep. In vain I seek the posture and simulate the gesture of an already favoured victim. I am too weak. I am too strong, yet I cannot rise and darken the room or go out and contemn sleep. It is a blessed thing if I am strong enough at last to wear myself out to sleep.

The other night I awoke just as the robin was beginning to sing outside in the dark garden. Beyond him the wind made a moan in the little fir-copse as of a forest in a space magically enclosed and silent, and in the intervals of his song silence fell about him like a cloak which the wind could not penetrate. As well as I knew the triple cry farther off for the crow of the first cock, I knew this for the robin's song, pausing but unbroken, though it was unlike any song of robin I had heard in daylight, standing or walking among trees. Outside, in the dark hush, to me lying prostrate, patient, unmoving, the song was absolutely monotonous, absolutely expressionless, a chain of little thin notes linked mechanically in a rhythm identical at each repetition. This was not the voluntary personal utterance of a winged sprite that I used to know, but a note touched on the instrument of night by a player unknown to me, save that it was he who delighted in the moaning fir-trees and in my silence. Nothing intelligible to me was expressed by it; since he, the player, alone knew, I call it expressionless.

When the light began to arrive, the song in the enclosed hush, and the sound of the trees beyond it, remained the same. I remained awake, silently and as stilly as possible, cringing for sleep. I was an unwilling note on the instrument; yet I do not know that the robin was less unwilling. I strove to escape out of that harmony of bird, wind, and man. But as fast as I made my mind a faintly heaving, shapeless, grey blank, some form of colour appeared; memory or anticipation was at work.

Gradually I found myself trying to understand this dawn harmony. I vowed to remember it and ponder it in the light of day. To make sure of remembering I tried putting it into rhyme. I was resolved not to omit the date; and so much so that the first line had to be 'The seventh of September', nor could I escape from this necessity. Then September was to be rhymed with. The word 'ember' occurred and stayed; no other would respond to all my calling. The third and fourth lines, it seemed, were bound to be something like –

The sere and the ember
Of the year and of me.

This gave me no satisfaction, but I was under a very strong compulsion. I could do no more; not a line would add itself to the wretched three; nor did they cease to return again and again to my head. It was fortunate for me as a man, if not as an unborn poet, that I could not forget the lines; for by continual helpless repetition of them I rose yet once more to the weakness that sleep demanded. Gradually I became conscious of nothing but the moan of the trees, the monotonous expressionless robin's song, the slightly aching body to which I was, by ties more and more slender, attached. I felt, I knew, I did not think that there would always be an unknown player, always wind and trees, always a robin singing, always a listener listening in the stark dawn: and I knew also that if I were the listener I should not always lie thus in a safe warm bed thinking myself alive. . . . And so I fell asleep again on the seventh of September.

The Last Sheaf, 39–43

Miscellanea, 1901–14

'The best lyrics seem to be the poet's natural speech'
   – *Daily Chronicle*, 27 August 1901

'About matters of the spirit, men are all engaged in colloquies with themselves. Some of them are overheard, and they are great poets.'
   – *Daily Chronicle*, 11 January 1904

'verse is the natural speech of men, as singing is of birds'
   – *The Week's Survey*, 18 June 1904

'We are now more than ever struck by the beauty of the ordinary speeches which, in their naturalness and real poetry, prove as much as Wordsworth's preface that the speech of poetry can be that of life.'
   – *Daily Chronicle*, 1 January 1907

'A great writer so uses the words of every day that they become a code of his own which the world is bound to learn and in the end take unto itself.'
   – *The South Country*, 1909

'The chief influences of our lives are unconscious, just as the best of our best work is'
   – *Feminine Influence on the Poets*, 1910

'A writer composes out of his experience, inward, outward and histrionic, or along the protracted lines of his experience.'
   – *George Borrow*, 1912

'No man, I suppose, can be "all ear" to a poem; he must stray a little now and then to think, apart from the tune.'
   – *Algernon Charles Swinburne*, 1912

'When a poet writes, I believe he is often only putting into words what such another old man puzzled out among the sheep in a long life-time.'
   – *The Country*, 1913

'It [literature] has to make words of such a spirit, and arrange them in such a manner, that they will do all that a speaker can do by innumerable gestures and their innumerable shades, by tone and pitch of voice, by speed, by pauses, by all that he is and all that he will become.'
   – *Walter Pater*, 1913

'a man will not easily write better than he speaks when some matter has touched him deeply'
   – *The New Weekly*, 8 August 1914

This England

Edward Thomas was in Dymock with Robert Frost when war broke out on 4 August 1914. An entry in his notebook from 26 August reads, 'a sky of dark rough horizontal masses in N.W. with a 1/3 moon bright and almost orange low down clear of cloud and I thought of men east-ward seeing it at the same moment. It seems foolish to have loved England up to now without knowing it could perhaps be ravaged and I could and perhaps would do nothing to prevent it' (FNB77, 26 August 1914, Berg). Those lines were revisited in what Thomas described to Frost as 'an article on the new moon of August 26 and you and me strolling about in the sun while our brave soldiers etc.' (letter, 19 November 1914, Dartmouth College). The article, 'This England', offered a unique glimpse into what Frost called their 'talks–walking' and became the genesis of Thomas's poem, 'The sun used to shine' (138), written the following year; in so doing, it began a defence of the English landscape that would eventually lead him to enlist.

It was a part of the country I had never known before, and I had no connections with it. Once only, during infancy, I had stayed here at a vicarage, and though I have been told things about it which it gives me, almost as if they were memories, a certain pleasure to recall, no genuine memory survives from the visit. All I can say is that the name, Hereford, had somehow won in my mind a very distinct meaning; it stood out among county names as the most delicately rustic of them all, with a touch of nobility given it long ago, I think, by Shakespeare's 'Harry of Hereford,

Lancaster, and Derby'. But now I was here for the third time since the year began. In April here I had heard, among apple trees in flower, not the first cuckoo, but the first abundance of day-long-calling cuckoos; here, the first nightingale's song, though too far-off and intermittently, twitched away by gusty night winds; here I found the earliest may-blossom which by May Day, while I still lingered, began to dapple the hedges thickly, and no rain fell, yet the land was sweet. Here I had the consummation of Midsummer, the weather radiant and fresh, yet hot and rainless, the white and the pink wild roses, the growing bracken, the last and best of the songs, blackbird's, blackcap's. Now it was August, and again no rain fell for many days; the harvest was a good one, and after standing long in the sun it was gathered in and put up in ricks in the sun, to the contentment of men and rooks. All day the rooks in the wheatfields were cawing a deep sweet caw, in alternating choirs or all together, almost like sheep bleating, contentedly, on until late evening. The sun shone, always warm, from skies sometimes cloudless, sometimes inscribed with a fine white scatter miles high, sometimes displaying the full pomp of white moving mountains, sometimes almost entirely shrouded in dull sulphurous threats, but vain ones.

Three meadows away lived a friend, and once or twice or three times a day I used to cross the meadows, the gate, and the two stiles. The first was a concave meadow, in April strewn with daffodils. There, day and night, pastured a bay colt and a black mare, thirty years old, but gay enough to have slipped away two years back and got herself made the mother of this 'stolen' foal. The path led across the middle of the meadow, through a gate, and alongside one of the hedges of the next, which sloped down rather steeply to the remnant of a brook, and was grazed by half a dozen cows.

At the bottom a hedge followed the line of the brook and a stile took me through it, with a deep drop, to a plank and a puddle, and so to the last field, a rough one. This rose up as steeply and was the night's lodging of four cart horses. The path, having gradually approached a hedge on the left, went alongside it, under the horse-chestnut tree leaning out of it, and in sight of the house, until it reached the far hedge and the road. There, at another stile, the path ceased. The little house of whitened bricks and black timbers lay a few yards up the road, a vegetable garden in front with a weeping ash and a bay-tree, a walnut in a yard of cobbles and grass behind, a yew on the roadside, an orchard on the other.

How easy it was to spend a morning or afternoon in walking over to this house, stopping to talk to whoever was about for a few minutes, and then strolling with my friend, nearly regardless of footpaths, in a long loop, so as to end either at his house or my lodging. It was mostly orchard and grass, gently up and down, seldom steep for more than a few yards. Some of the meadows had a group or a line of elms; one an ash rising out of an islet of dense brambles; many had several great old apple or pear trees. The pears were small brown perry pears, as thick as haws, the apples chiefly cider apples, innumerable, rosy and uneatable, though once or twice we did pick up a wasp's remnant, with slightly greasy skin of palest yellow, that tasted delicious. There was one brook to cross, shallow and leaden, with high hollow bare banks. More than one meadow was trenched, apparently by a dried watercourse, showing flags, rushes, and a train of willows.

If talk dwindled in the traversing of a big field, the pause at gate or stile braced it again. Often we prolonged the pause, whether we actually sat or not, and we talked – of flowers, childhood, Shakespeare, women, England, the war – or we looked at a far horizon, which some dip or gap occasionally disclosed. Again and again we saw, instead of solid things, dark or bright, never more than half a mile off, the complete broad dome of a high hill six miles distant, a beautiful hill itself, but especially seen thus, always unexpectedly, through gaps in this narrow country, as through a window. Moreover, we knew that from the summit, between the few old Scots firs and the young ones of the plantation, we could command the Severn and the Cotswolds on the one hand, and on the other the Wye, the Forest of Dean, the island hills of North Monmouthshire, dark and massive, the remote Black Mountains pale and cloud-like, far beyond them in Wales. Not that we often needed to escape from this narrow country, or that, if we did, we had to look so far. For example, the cloud and haze of a hot day would change all. As we sat on a gate, the elms in a near hedge grew sombre, though clear. Past them rose a field like a low pitched roof dotted over with black stooks of beans and the elms at the top of that rise looked black and ponderous. Those in farther hedges were dimmer and less heavy, some were as puffs of smoke, while just below the long straight ridge of the horizon, a mile or two away, the trees were no more than the shadows of smoke.

Lombardy poplars rose out from among the elms, near and far, in twos and threes, in longer or shorter lines, and at one point grouping themselves like the pinnacles of a cathedral. Most farm-houses in the neighbourhood, and even pairs of cottages, possessed a couple or more. If we got astray we could steer by this or that high-perched cluster, in which, perhaps, one tree having lost a branch now on one side, now on the other, resembled a grass stalk with flowers alternating up it. When night came on, any farmhouse group might be transmuted out of all knowledge, partly with the aid of its Lombardy poplars. There was also one tree without a house which looked magnificent at that hour. It stood alone, except for a much lesser tree, as it were, kneeling at its feet, on the long swooping curve of a great meadow against the sky; and when the curve and the two trees upon it were clear black under a pale sky and the first stars, they made a kind of naturally dramatic 'C'est l'empereur' scene, such as must be as common as painters in a cypress country.

Whatever road or lane we took, once in every quarter of a mile we came to a farm-house. Only there by the two trees we tasted austere inhuman solitude as a luxury. Yet a man had planted the trees fifty or sixty years back. (Who was it, I wonder, set the fashion or distributed the seed-lings?) It was really not less human a scene than that other one I liked at nightfall. Wildly dark clouds broke through the pallid sky above the elms, shadowy elms towering up ten times their diurnal height; and under the trees stood a thatched cottage, sending up a thin blue smoke against the foliage, and casting a faint light out from one square win-dow and open door. It was cheerful and mysterious too. No man of any nation accustomed to houses but must have longed for his home at the sight, or have suffered for lack-ing one, or have dreamed that this was it.

Then one evening the new moon made a difference. It was the end of a wet day; at least, it had begun wet, had turned warm and muggy, and at last fine but still cloudy. The sky was banded with rough masses in the north-west, but the moon, a stout orange crescent, hung free of cloud near the horizon. At one stroke, I thought, like many other people, what things that same new moon sees eastward about the Meuse in France. Of those who could see it there, not blinded by smoke, pain, or excitement, how many saw it and heeded? I was deluged, in a second stroke, by another thought, or something that overpowered thought. All I can tell is, it seemed to me that either I had never loved England, or I had loved it foolishly, aesthetically, like a slave, not having realized that it was not mine unless I were willing and prepared to die rather than leave it as Belgian women and old men and children had left their country. Something I had omitted. Something, I felt, had to be done before I could look again composedly at English landscape, at the elms and poplars about the houses, at the purple-headed wood-betony with two pairs of dark leaves on a stiff stem, who stood sentinel among the grasses or bracken by hedge-side or wood's-edge. What he stood sentinel for I did not know, any more than what I had got to do.

The Nation, vol. 16, no. 6, 7 November 1914, 170–1, repr. in *The Last Sheaf*, 215–21

The White Horse

In a notebook from 1914, beside an entry dated 2 November, Thomas roughed a dozen lines that began, 'I could wring the old girl's neck | That put it here | A public house! (Charcoal burner)' (FNB 79, October–December 1914, Berg). The notes formed the basis of a prose piece, 'The White Horse', drafted on 16 November, set in the inn of that name on the Froxfield Plateau above Steep. It was from this draft that Thomas drew his first poem, 'Up in the Wind' (45), in the weeks that immediately followed.

Tall beeches overhang the inn, dwarfing and half hiding it, for it lies back a field's breadth from the by road. The field is divided from the r[oa]d by a hedge and only a path fr[om] one corner and a cart track fr the other which meet under the beeches connect the inn with the rd. But for a signboard or rather the post and empty iron frame of a signboard close to the road behind the hedge a traveller c[oul]d not guess it an inn. The low dirty white bdg [building] looks like a farmhouse, with a lean-to, a rick and a shed of black boarding at one side; and in fact the landlord is more than half farmer. Except from the cottages which are scattered far around, only one of them visible fr the inn, customers are few. And yet it is almost at a crossing of roads. One field away from the field w[ith] the signpost the byroad crosses a main rd at a high p[oin]t on the table land: the inn itself stands so high that its beeches mark it for those who know and form a station for the eyes of strangers, many miles away on 3 sides. But both roads lack houses and the travellers, especially on the main rd, are motorists fr the ends of the earth and farmers going to market fr remote villages. The main road runs for one length of 4 m[iles] without a house of any sort; once the land was all common. Many acres of it are still possessed by gorse and inhabited chiefly by linnets and a pair of stone curlews. The name of common clings to it tho[ugh] it is hedged. Gorse and bracken mingle with the hedgerow hawthorn and keep memories of the old waste alive. Few trees of any age stand alongside the rd, and as the hedges are low and broken, and everywhere gorse is visible, even the stranger has whiffs of the past and tastes something like the olden sensation of journeying over wide common, high and unpopulated, higher than anything except Butser Hill far behind him and the Inkpen far before him northward.

The farmhouses naturally then are placed far back behind the gorse or the fields once belonging to it and are reached by lanes of various lengths out of the main rd. Once, I think, the roads crossed in the midst of a wide tract of common which perhaps ended where now the inn is. But as things are it m[igh]t well will [*sic*] seem to have been hidden there out of someone's perversity. 'I sh[oul]d like to wring the old girl's neck for coming away here.' So said the woman who fetched my beer when I found myself at the inn first. She was a daughter of the house, fresh from a long absence in service in London, a bright wildish slattern with a cockney accent and her hair half down. She spoke angrily. If she did not get away before long, she said, she w[oul]d go mad with the loneliness. She looked out sharply: all she cd see was the beeches and the tiny pond beneath them and the calves standing in it drinking, alternately grazing the water here and there and thinking, and at last going out and standing still on the bank thinking. Who the 'old girl' was, whether she had built the house here, or what, I did not inquire. It was just the loneliness of the high placed little inn isolated under those tall beeches that pleased me. Every year I used to go there once or twice, never so often as to overcome the original feeling it had given me. I was always on the verge of turning that feeling of having it turned by a natural process, into a story. Whoever the characters wd have been I do not think they wd have included either the 'old girl' or the landlord's indignant cockney daughter. The story that was to interpret the look that the house had as you came up to it under the trees never took shape. The daughter stayed on several yrs, bearing it so well that her wildish looks and cockney accent seemed to fit the scene and I used to look forward to meeting her again. She wd come in with her hair halfdown as at first or I would find her scrubbing the bricks or getting dinner ready in the taproom which was kitchen also. But before I had learnt anything from her she went. I have to be content with what the landlord told me yrs afterwards, when he left his wheelbarrow standing in profile like a pig and came in to his taproom out of his fmyd [farmyard] for a glass and stood drinking outside the door.

Originally or as far back as he knew of, the house was a blacksmith's, the lean-to taproom was the smithy as you can tell by the height of it, and the man was remembered and still spoken of for his skill. The landlord spoke of him yet had never seen him. The smith died and left a widow and as she cd not use hammer and tongs and as no 2nd smith arrived to marry her, she turned the smithy into a shop and had an off licence to sell beer. Presently a man came along from the Chiltern beech country with a two-cylinder engine for sawing timber. At that day the land here carried far more woodland. The beech trunks were cut up to make chairs. The branches were burned for charcoal, and the circular black floors of the charcoal burner's fires are still now and then cut into by the farmer's plough. The man fr the Chilterns came here to saw beech planks and brought with him a little boy, his nephew, who had to pick up chips to feed the fire of the engine. 'My uncle' said the landlord 'fell in love, I suppose, with the widow and married her.' He continued to go about the country with his engine sawing timber. But the beeches overhanging the house were spared. The boy stayed on and farmed. The shop was turned into a taproom with a full licence, and the widow sold ale until she died. The man grew old and gave up sawing and then he died. Now the nephew farms the land. It is worth a guinea a mile he says, but he has grown fat on the beer which his daughters draw. On the wall of the taproom is a list of the officers of a slate club and also coloured diagrams illustrating certain diseases of the cow. The room smells as much of bacon and boiled vegetables as of ale and shag, and it is often silent and empty except for a painted wooden clock ticking loudly above the fire. Yet it is one of the pleasantest rooms in Hampshire, well deserving the footpaths which lead men to it from all directions over ploughland and meadow, and deserving as good a story as a man could write.

Old Man's Beard

'*Old Man* scent,' Thomas wrote in his notebook on 11 November 1914, 'I smell again and again not really liking it but venerating it because it holds the secret of something very long ago which I feel it may someday recall, but I have got no idea what' (FNB 79, Berg). A few days later, on 17 November 1914, Thomas roughed out the prose sketch below that on 6 December became the verse draft of 'Old Man' (51).

Just as she is turning in to the house or leaving it, the baby plucks a feather of old man's beard. The bush grows just across the path fr[om] the door. Sometimes she stands by it squeezing off tip after tip from the branches and shrivelling them between her fingers on to the path in grey-green shreds. So the bush is still only half as tall as she is, though it is the same age. She never talks of it, but I wonder how much of the garden she will remember, the hedge with the old damson trees topping it, the vegetable rows, the path bending round the house corner, the old man's beard opposite the door, and me sometimes forbidding her to touch it, if she lives to my years. As for myself I cannot remember when I first smelt that green bitterness. I, too, often gather a sprig fr the bush and sniff it, and roll it between my fingers and sniff again and think, trying to discover what it is that I am remembering. I do not wholly like the smell, yet w[oul]d rather lose many meaningless sweeter ones than this bitter one of which I have mislaid the key. As I hold the sprig to my nose and slowly withdraw it I think of nothing, I see, I hear nothing; yet I seem too to be listening, lying in wait for whatever it is I ought to remember but never do. No garden comes back to me, no hedge or path, no grey-green bush called old man's beard or lad's love, no figure of mother or father or playmate, only a dark avenue without an end.

Lockwood Memorial Library

Up in the Wind

'I could wring the old thing's neck that put it here!
A public-house! it may be public for birds,
Squirrels and such-like, ghosts of charcoal-burners
And highwaymen.' The wild girl laughed. 'But I
Hate it since I came back from Kennington.
I gave up a good place.' Her Cockney accent
Made her and the house seem wilder by calling up –
Only to be subdued at once by wildness –
The idea of London, there in that forest parlour,
Low and small among the towering beeches
And the one bulging butt that's like a font.

Her eyes flashed up; she shook her hair away
From eyes and mouth, as if to shriek again;
Then sighed back to her scrubbing. While I drank
I might have mused of coaches and highwaymen,
Charcoal-burners and life that loves the wild.
For who now used these roads except myself,
A market waggon every other Wednesday,
A solitary tramp, some very fresh one
Ignorant of these eleven houseless miles,
A motorist from a distance slowing down
To taste whatever luxury he can
In having North Downs clear behind, South clear before,
And being midway between two railway lines
Far out of sight or sound of them? There are
Some houses – down the by-lanes; and a few
Are visible – when their damsons are in bloom.

But the land is wild, and there's a spirit of wildness
Much older, crying when the stone-curlew yodels
His sea and mountain cry, high up in Spring.
He nests in fields where still the gorse is free as
When all was open and common. Common 'tis named
And calls itself, because the bracken and gorse
Still hold the hedge where plough and scythe have
    chased them.
Once on a time 'tis plain that 'The White Horse'
Stood merely on the border of a waste
Where horse or cart picked its own course afresh.
On all sides then, as now, paths ran to the inn;
And now a farm-track takes you from a gate.

Two roads cross, and not a house in sight
Except 'The White Horse' in this clump of beeches.
It hides from either road, a field's breadth back;
And it's the trees you see, and not the house,
Both near and far, when the clump's the highest thing
And homely, too, upon a far horizon
To one that knows there is an inn within.

''Twould have been different,' the wild girl shrieked,
    'suppose
That widow had married another blacksmith and
Kept on the business. This parlour was the smithy.
If she had done, there might never have been an inn
And I, in that case, might never have been born.
Years ago, when this was all a wood
And the smith had charcoal-burners for company,
A man from a beech-country in the shires
Came with an engine and a little boy
(To feed the engine) to cut up timber here.

[46]

It all happened years ago. The smith
Had died, his widow had set up an alehouse –
I could wring the old thing's neck for thinking of it.
Well, I suppose they fell in love, the widow
And my great-uncle that sawed up the timber:
Leastways they married. The little boy stayed on.
He was my father.' She thought she'd scrub again –
'I draw the ale and he grows fat' she muttered –
But only studied the hollows in the bricks
And chose among her thoughts in stirring silence.
The clock ticked, and the big saucepan lid
Heaved as the cabbage bubbled, and the girl
Questioned the fire and spoke: 'My father, he
Took to the land. A mile of it is worth
A guinea; for by that time all the trees
Except these few about the house were gone:
That's all that's left of the forest unless you count
The bottoms of the charcoal-burners' fires –
We plough one up at times. Did you ever see
Our signboard?' No. The post and empty frame
I knew. Without them I should not have guessed
The low grey house and its one stack under trees
Was a public house and not a hermitage.
'But can that empty frame be any use?
Now I should like to see a good white horse
Swing there, a really beautiful white horse,
Galloping one side, being painted on the other.'
'But would you like to hear it swing all night
And all day? All I ever had to thank
The wind for was for blowing the sign down.
Time after time it blew down and I could sleep.
At last they fixed it, and it took a thief
To move it, and we've never had another:

It's lying at the bottom of the pond.
But no one's moved the wood from off the hill
There at the back, although it makes a noise
When the wind blows; as if a train were running
The other side, a train that never stops
Or ends. And the linen crackles on the line
Like a wood fire rising.' 'But if you had the sign
You might draw company. What about Kennington?'
She bent down to her scrubbing with 'Not me:
Not back to Kennington. Here I was born,
And I've a notion on these windy nights
Here I shall die. Perhaps I want to die here.
I reckon I shall stay. But I do wish
The road was nearer and the wind farther off,
Or once now and then quite still, though when I die
I'd have it blowing that I might go with it
Somewhere distant, where there are trees no more
And I could wake and not know where I was
Nor even wonder if they would roar again.
Look at those calves.'
                              Between the open door
And the trees two calves were wading in the pond,
Grazing the water here and there and thinking,
Sipping and thinking, both happily, neither long.
The water wrinkled, but they sipped and thought,
As careless of the wind as it of us.
'Look at those calves. Hark at the trees again.'

March

Now I know that Spring will come again,
Perhaps tomorrow: however late I've patience
After this night following on such a day.

While still my temples ached from the cold burning
Of hail and wind, and still the primroses
Torn by the hail were covered up in it,
The sun filled earth and heaven with a great light
And a tenderness, almost warmth, where the hail
    dripped,
As if the mighty sun wept tears of joy.
But 'twas too late for warmth. The sunset piled
Mountains on mountains of snow and ice in the west:
Somewhere among their folds the wind was lost,
And yet 'twas cold, and though I knew that Spring
Would come again, I knew it had not come,
That it was lost too in those mountains chill.

What did the thrushes know? Rain, snow, sleet, hail,
Had kept them quiet as the primroses.
They had but an hour to sing. On boughs they sang,
On gates, on ground; they sang while they changed
    perches
And while they fought, if they remembered to fight:
So earnest were they to pack into that hour
Their unwilling hoard of song before the moon
Grew brighter than the clouds. Then 'twas no time
For singing merely. So they could keep off silence

And night, they cared not what they sang or screamed;
Whether 'twas hoarse or sweet or fierce or soft;
And to me all was sweet: they could do no wrong.
Something they knew – I also, while they sang
And after. Not till night had half its stars
And never a cloud, was I aware of silence
Stained with all that hour's songs, a silence
Saying that Spring returns, perhaps tomorrow.

Old Man

Old Man, or Lad's-love, – in the name there's nothing
To one that knows not Lad's-love, or Old Man,
The hoar-green feathery herb, almost a tree,
Growing with rosemary and lavender.
Even to one that knows it well, the names
Half decorate, half perplex, the thing it is:
At least, what that is clings not to the names
In spite of time. And yet I like the names.

The herb itself I like not, but for certain
I love it, as some day the child will love it
Who plucks a feather from the door-side bush
Whenever she goes in or out of the house.
Often she waits there, snipping the tips and shrivelling
The shreds at last on to the path, perhaps
Thinking, perhaps of nothing, till she sniffs
Her fingers and runs off. The bush is still
But half as tall as she, though it is as old;
So well she clips it. Not a word she says;
And I can only wonder how much hereafter
She will remember, with that bitter scent,
Of garden rows, and ancient damson-trees
Topping a hedge, a bent path to a door,
A low thick bush beside the door, and me
Forbidding her to pick.

                         As for myself,
Where first I met the bitter scent is lost.

I, too, often shrivel the grey shreds,
Sniff them and think and sniff again and try
Once more to think what it is I am remembering,
Always in vain. I cannot like the scent,
Yet I would rather give up others more sweet,
With no meaning, than this bitter one.

I have mislaid the key. I sniff the spray
And think of nothing; I see and I hear nothing;
Yet seem, too, to be listening, lying in wait
For what I should, yet never can, remember:
No garden appears, no path, no hoar-green bush
Of Lad's-love, or Old Man, no child beside,
Neither father nor mother, nor any playmate;
Only an avenue, dark, nameless, without end.

The Signpost

The dim sea glints chill. The white sun is shy.
And the skeleton weeds and the never-dry,
Rough, long grasses keep white with frost
At the hilltop by the finger-post;
The smoke of the traveller's-joy is puffed
Over hawthorn berry and hazel tuft.

I read the sign. Which way shall I go?
A voice says: You would not have doubted so
At twenty. Another voice gentle with scorn
Says: At twenty you wished you had never been born.

One hazel lost a leaf of gold
From a tuft at the tip, when the first voice told
The other he wished to know what 'twould be
To be sixty by this same post. 'You shall see,'
He laughed – and I had to join his laughter –
'You shall see; but either before or after,
Whatever happens, it must befall,
A mouthful of earth to remedy all
Regrets and wishes shall freely be given;
And if there be a flaw in that heaven
'Twill be freedom to wish, and your wish may be
To be here or anywhere talking to me,
No matter what the weather, on earth,
At any age between death and birth, –
To see what day or night can be,
The sun and the frost, the land and the sea,

Summer, Autumn, Winter, Spring, –
With a poor man of any sort, down to a king,
Standing upright out in the air
Wondering where he shall journey, O where?'

The Other

The forest ended. Glad I was
To feel the light, and hear the hum
Of bees, and smell the drying grass
And the sweet mint, because I had come
To an end of forest, and because
Here was both road and inn, the sum
Of what's not forest. But 'twas here
They asked me if I did not pass
Yesterday this way? 'Not you? Queer.'
'Who then? and slept here?' I felt fear.

I learnt his road and, ere they were
Sure I was I, left the dark wood
Behind, kestrel and woodpecker,
The inn in the sun, the happy mood
When first I tasted sunlight there.
I travelled fast, in hopes I should
Outrun that other. What to do
When caught, I planned not. I pursued
To prove the likeness, and, if true,
To watch until myself I knew.

I tried the inns that evening
Of a long gabled high-street grey,
Of courts and outskirts, travelling
An eager but a weary way,
In vain. He was not there. Nothing
Told me that ever till that day

Had one like me entered those doors,
Save once. That time I dared: 'You may
Recall' – but never-foamless shores
Make better friends than those dull boors.

Many and many a day like this
Aimed at the unseen moving goal
And nothing found but remedies
For all desire. These made not whole;
They sowed a new desire, to kiss
Desire's self beyond control,
Desire of desire. And yet
Life stayed on within my soul.
One night in sheltering from the wet
I quite forgot I could forget.

A customer, then the landlady
Stared at me. With a kind of smile
They hesitated awkwardly:
Their silence gave me time for guile.
Had anyone called there like me,
I asked. It was quite plain the wile
Succeeded. For they poured out all.
And that was naught. Less than a mile
Beyond the inn, I could recall
He was like me in general.

He had pleased them, but I less.
I was more eager than before
To find him out and to confess,
To bore him and to let him bore.
I could not wait: children might guess
I had a purpose, something more

That made an answer indiscreet.
One girl's caution made me sore,
Too indignant even to greet
That other had we chanced to meet.

I sought then in solitude.
The wind had fallen with the night; as still
The roads lay as the ploughland rude,
Dark and naked, on the hill.
Had there been ever any feud
'Twixt earth and sky, a mighty will
Closed it: the crocketed dark trees,
A dark house, dark impossible
Cloud-towers, one star, one lamp, one peace
Held on an everlasting lease:

And all was earth's, or all was sky's;
No difference endured between
The two. A dog barked on a hidden rise;
A marshbird whistled high unseen;
The latest waking blackbird's cries
Perished upon the silence keen.
The last light filled a narrow firth
Among the clouds. I stood serene,
And with a solemn quiet mirth,
An old inhabitant of earth.

Once the name I gave to hours
Like this was melancholy, when
It was not happiness and powers
Coming like exiles home again,
And weaknesses quitting their bowers,
Smiled and enjoyed, far off from men,

Moments of everlastingness.
And fortunate my search was then
While what I sought, nevertheless,
That I was seeking, I did not guess.

That time was brief: once more at inn
And upon road I sought my man
Till once amid a tap-room's din
Loudly he asked for me, began
To speak, as if it had been a sin,
Of how I thought and dreamed and ran
After him thus, day after day:
He lived as one under a ban
For this: what had I got to say?
I said nothing, I slipped away.

And now I dare not follow after
Too close. I try to keep in sight,
Dreading his frown and worse his laughter.
I steal out of the wood to light;
I see the swift shoot from the rafter
By the inn door: ere I alight
I wait and hear the starlings wheeze
And nibble like ducks: I wait his flight.
He goes: I follow: no release
Until he ceases. Then I also shall cease.

The Mountain Chapel

Chapel and gravestones, old and few,
Are shrouded by a mountain fold
From sound and view
Of life. The loss of the brook's voice
Falls like a shadow. All they hear is
The eternal noise
Of wind whistling in grass more shrill
Than aught as human as a sword,
And saying still:
''Tis but a moment since man's birth,
And in another moment more
Man lies in earth
For ever; but I am the same
Now, and shall be, even as I was
Before he came:
Till there is nothing I shall be.'

Yet there the sun shines after noon
So cheerfully
The place almost seems peopled, nor
Lacks cottage chimney, cottage hearth:
It is not more
In size than is a cottage, less
Than any other empty home
In homeliness.
It has a garden of wild flowers
And finest grass and gravestones warm
In sunshine hours

The year through. Men behind the glass
Stand once a week, singing, and drown
The whistling grass
Their ponies munch. And yet somewhere,
Near or far off, there's some man could
Live happy here,
Or one of the gods perhaps, were they
Not of inhuman stature dire,
As poets say
Who have not seen them clearly; if
At sound of any wind of the world
In grass-blades stiff
They would not startle and shudder cold
Under the sun. When gods were young
This wind was old.

The Manor Farm

The rock-like mud unfroze a little and rills
Ran and sparkled down each side of the road
Under the catkins wagging in the hedge.
But earth would have her sleep out, spite of the sun;
Nor did I value that thin gilding beam
More than a pretty February thing
Till I came down to the old Manor Farm,
And church and yew-tree opposite, in age
Its equals and in size. The church and yew
And farmhouse slept in a Sunday silentness.
The air raised not a straw. The steep farm roof,
With tiles duskily glowing, entertained
The mid-day sun; and up and down the roof
White pigeons nestled. There was no sound but one.
Three cart-horses were looking over a gate
Drowsily through their forelocks, swishing their tails
Against a fly, a solitary fly.

The Winter's cheek flushed as if he had drained
Spring, Summer, and Autumn at a draught
And smiled quietly. But 'twas not Winter –
Rather a season of bliss unchangeable
Awakened from farm and church where it had lain
Safe under tile and thatch for ages since
This England, Old already, was called Merry.

An Old Song

I was not apprenticed nor ever dwelt in famous Lincolnshire;
I've served one master ill and well much more than seven
  year;
And never took up to poaching as you shall quickly find;
 But 'tis my delight of a shiny night in the season of
  the year.

I roamed where nobody had a right but keepers and squires,
  and there
I sought for nests, wild flowers, oak sticks, and moles, both
  far and near,
And had to run from farmers, and learnt the Lincolnshire
  song:
 'Oh, 'tis my delight of a shiny night in the season of
  the year.'

I took those walks years after, talking with friend or dear,
Or solitary musing; but when the moon shone clear
I had no joy or sorrow that could not be expressed
 By ''Tis my delight of a shiny night in the season of
  the year.'

Since then I've thrown away a chance to fight a gamekeeper;
And I less often trespass, and what I see or hear
Is mostly from the road or path by day: yet still I sing:
 'Oh, 'tis my delight of a shiny night in the season of
  the year.'

For if I am contented, at home or anywhere,
Or if I sigh for I know not what, or my heart beats with
      some fear,
It is a strange kind of delight to sing or whistle just:
    'Oh, 'tis my delight of a shiny night in the season of
      the year.'

And with this melody on my lips and no one by to care,
Indoors, or out on shiny nights or dark in open air,
I am for a moment made a man that sings out of his heart:
    'Oh, 'tis my delight of a shiny night in the season of
      the year.'

The Combe

The Combe was ever dark, ancient and dark.
Its mouth is stopped with bramble, thorn, and briar;
And no one scrambles over the sliding chalk
By beech and yew and perishing juniper
Down the half precipices of its sides, with roots
And rabbit holes for steps. The sun of Winter,
The moon of Summer, and all the singing birds
Except the missel-thrush that loves juniper,
Are quite shut out. But far more ancient and dark
The Combe looks since they killed the badger there,
Dug him out and gave him to the hounds,
That most ancient Briton of English beasts.

The New Year

He was the one man I met up in the woods
That stormy New Year's morning; and at first sight,
Fifty yards off, I could not tell how much
Of the strange tripod was a man. His body,
Bowed horizontal, was supported equally
By legs at one end, by a rake at the other:
Thus he rested, far less like a man than
His wheel-barrow in profile was like a pig.
But when I saw it was an old man bent,
At the same moment came into my mind
The games at which boys bend thus, *High-Cockalorum*,
Or *Fly-the-garter*, and *Leap-frog*. At the sound
Of footsteps he began to straighten himself;
His head rolled under his cape like a tortoise's;
He took an unlit pipe out of his mouth
Politely ere I wished him 'A Happy New Year',
And with his head cast upward sideways muttered –
So far as I could hear through the trees' roar –
'Happy New Year, and may it come fastish, too,'
While I strode by and he turned to raking leaves.

Snow

In the gloom of whiteness,
In the great silence of snow,
A child was sighing
And bitterly saying: 'Oh,
They have killed a white bird up there on her nest,
The down is fluttering from her breast.'
And still it fell through that dusky brightness
On the child crying for the bird of the snow.

Adlestrop

Yes. I remember Adlestrop –
The name, because one afternoon
Of heat the express-train drew up there
Unwontedly. It was late June.

The steam hissed. Someone cleared his throat.
No one left and no one came
On the bare platform. What I saw
Was Adlestrop – only the name

And willows, willow-herb, and grass,
And meadowsweet, and haycocks dry,
No whit less still and lonely fair
Than the high cloudlets in the sky.

And for that minute a blackbird sang
Close by, and round him, mistier,
Farther and farther, all the birds
Of Oxfordshire and Gloucestershire.

Over the Hills

Often and often it came back again
To mind, the day I passed the horizon ridge
To a new country, the path I had to find
By half-gaps that were stiles once in the hedge,
The pack of scarlet clouds running across
The harvest evening that seemed endless then
And after, and the inn where all were kind,
All were strangers. I did not know my loss
Till one day twelve months later suddenly
I leaned upon my spade and saw it all,
Though far beyond the sky-line. It became
Almost a habit through the year for me
To lean and see it and think to do the same
Again for two days and a night. Recall
Was vain: no more could the restless brook
Ever turn back and climb the waterfall
To the lake that rests and stirs not in its nook,
As in the hollow of the collar-bone
Under the mountain's head of rush and stone.

Man and Dog

"'Twill take some getting.' 'Sir, I think 'twill so.'
The old man stared up at the mistletoe
That hung too high in the poplar's crest for plunder
Of any climber, though not for kissing under:
Then he went on against the north-east wind –
Straight but lame, leaning on a staff new-skinned,
Carrying a brolly, flag-basket, and old coat, –
Towards Alton, ten miles off. And he had not
Done less from Chilgrove where he pulled up docks.
'Twere best, if he had had 'a money-box',
To have waited there till the sheep cleared a field
For what a half-week's flint-picking would yield.
His mind was running on the work he had done
Since he left Christchurch in the New Forest, one
Spring in the 'seventies, – navvying on dock and line
From Southampton to Newcastle-on-Tyne, –
In 'seventy-four a year of soldiering
With the Berkshires, – hoeing and harvesting
In half the shires where corn and couch will grow.
His sons, three sons, were fighting, but the hoe
And reap-hook he liked, or anything to do with trees.
He fell once from a poplar tall as these:
The Flying Man they called him in hospital.
'If I flew now, to another world I'd fall.'
He laughed and whistled to the small brown bitch
With spots of blue that hunted in the ditch.
Her foxy Welsh grandfather must have paired
Beneath him. He kept sheep in Wales and scared

Strangers, I will warrant, with his pearl eye
And trick of shrinking off as he were shy,
Then following close in silence for – for what?
'No rabbit, never fear, she ever got,
Yet always hunts. To-day she nearly had one:
She would and she wouldn't. 'Twas like that. The
    bad one!
She's not much use, but still she's company,
Though I'm not. She goes everywhere with me.
So Alton I must reach to-night somehow:
I'll get no shakedown with that bedfellow
From farmers. Many a man sleeps worse to-night
Than I shall.' 'In the trenches.' 'Yes, that's right.
But they'll be out of that – I hope they be –
This weather, marching after the enemy.'
'And so I hope. Good luck.' And there I nodded
'Good-night. You keep straight on.' Stiffly he plodded;
And at his heels the crisp leaves scurried fast,
And the leaf-coloured robin watched. They passed,
The robin till next day, the man for good,
Together in the twilight of the wood.

Beauty

What does it mean? Tired, angry, and ill at ease,
No man, woman, or child, alive could please
Me now. And yet I almost dare to laugh
Because I sit and frame an epitaph –
'Here lies all that no one loved of him
And that loved no one.' Then in a trice that whim
Has wearied. But, though I am like a river
At fall of evening while it seems that never
Has the sun lighted it or warmed it, while
Cross breezes cut the surface to a file,
This heart, some fraction of me, happily
Floats through the window even now to a tree
Down in the misting, dim-lit, quiet vale,
Not like a pewit that returns to wail
For something it has lost, but like a dove
That slants unswerving to its home and love.
There I find my rest, as through the dusk air
Flies what yet lives in me: Beauty is there.

First known when lost

I never had noticed it until
'Twas gone, – the narrow copse
Where now the woodman lops
The last of the willows with his bill.

It was not more than a hedge overgrown.
One meadow's breadth away
I passed it day by day.
Now the soil was bare as a bone,

And black betwixt two meadows green,
Though fresh-cut faggot ends
Of hazel made some amends
With a gleam as if flowers they had been.

Strange it could have hidden so near!
And now I see as I look
That the small winding brook,
A tributary's tributary, rises there.

The Owl

Downhill I came, hungry, and yet not starved;
Cold, yet had heat within me that was proof
Against the North wind; tired, yet so that rest
Had seemed the sweetest thing under a roof.

Then at the inn I had food, fire, and rest,
Knowing how hungry, cold, and tired was I.
All of the night was quite barred out except
An owl's cry, a most melancholy cry

Shaken out long and clear upon the hill,
No merry note, nor cause of merriment,
But one telling me plain what I escaped
And others could not, that night, as in I went.

And salted was my food, and my repose,
Salted and sobered, too, by the bird's voice
Speaking for all who lay under the stars,
Soldiers and poor, unable to rejoice.

The Bridge

I have come a long way today:
On a strange bridge alone,
Remembering friends, old friends,
I rest, without smile or moan,
As they remember me without smile or moan.

All are behind, the kind
And the unkind too, no more
To-night than a dream. The stream
Runs softly yet drowns the Past,
The dark-lit stream has drowned the Future
  and the Past.

No traveller has rest more blest
Than this moment brief between
Two lives, when the Night's first lights
And shades hide what has never been,
Things goodlier, lovelier, dearer, than will be
  or have been.

Good-night

The skylarks are far behind that sang over the down;
I can hear no more those suburb nightingales;
Thrushes and blackbirds sing in the gardens of the town
In vain: the noise of man, beast, and machine prevails.

But the call of children in the unfamiliar streets
That echo with a familiar twilight echoing,
Sweet as the voice of nightingale or lark, completes
A magic of strange welcome, so that I seem a king

Among man, beast, machine, bird, child, and the ghost
That in the echo lives and with the echo dies.
The friendless town is friendly; homeless, I not lost;
Though I know none of these doors, and meet but
    strangers' eyes.

Never again, perhaps, after tomorrow, shall
I see these homely streets, these church windows alight,
Not a man or woman or child among them all:
But it is All Friends' Night, a traveller's good night.

But these things also

But these things also are Spring's –
On banks by the roadside the grass
Long-dead that is greyer now
Than all the Winter it was;

The shell of a little snail bleached
In the grass; chip of flint, and mite
Of chalk; and the small birds' dung
In splashes of purest white:

All the white things a man mistakes
For earliest violets
Who seeks through Winter's ruins
Something to pay Winter's debts,

While the North blows, and starling flocks
By chattering on and on
Keep their spirits up in the mist,
And Spring's here, Winter's not gone.

The Path

Running along a bank, a parapet
That saves from the precipitous wood below
The level road, there is a path. It serves
Children for looking down the long smooth steep,
Between the legs of beech and yew, to where
A fallen tree checks the sight: while men and women
Content themselves with the road and what they see
Over the bank, and what the children tell.
The path, winding like silver, trickles on,
Bordered and even invaded by thinnest moss
That tries to cover roots and crumbling chalk
With gold, olive, and emerald, but in vain.
The children wear it. They have flattened the bank
On top, and silvered it between the moss
With the current of their feet, year after year.
But the road is houseless, and leads not to school.
To see a child is rare there, and the eye
Has but the road, the wood that overhangs
And underyawns it, and the path that looks
As if it led on to some legendary
Or fancied place where men have wished to go
And stay; till, sudden, it ends where the wood ends.

Wind and Mist

They met inside the gateway that gives the view,
A hollow land as vast as heaven. 'It is
A pleasant day, sir.' 'A very pleasant day.'
'And what a view here. If you like angled fields
Of grass and grain bounded by oak and thorn,
Here is a league. Had we with Germany
To play upon this board it could not be
More dear than April has made it with a smile.
The fields beyond that league close in together
And merge, even as our days into the past,
Into one wood that has a shining pane
Of water. Then the hills of the horizon –
That is how I should make hills had I to show
One who would never see them what hills were like.'
'Yes. Sixty miles of South Downs at one glance.
Sometimes a man feels proud at them, as if
He had just created them with one mighty thought.'
'That house, though modern, could not be better planned
For its position. I never liked a new
House better. Could you tell me who lives in it?'
'No one.' 'Ah – and I was peopling all
Those windows on the south with happy eyes,
The terrace under them with happy feet;
Girls –' 'Sir, I know. I know. I have seen that house
Through mist look lovely as a castle in Spain,
And airier. I have thought: "'Twere happy there
To live." And I have laughed at that
Because I lived there then.' 'Extraordinary.'

'Yes, with my furniture and family
Still in it, I, knowing every nook of it
And loving none, and in fact hating it.'
'Dear me! How could that be? But pardon me.'
'No offence. Doubtless the house was not to blame,
But the eye watching from those windows saw,
Many a day, day after day, mist – mist
Like chaos surging back – and felt itself
Alone in all the world, marooned alone.
We lived in clouds, on a cliff's edge almost
(You see), and if clouds went, the visible earth
Lay too far off beneath and like a cloud.
I did not know it was the earth I loved
Until I tried to live there in the clouds
And the earth turned to cloud.' 'You had a garden
Of flint and clay, too.' 'True; that was real enough.
The flint was the one crop that never failed.
The clay first broke my heart, and then my back;
And the back heals not. There were other things
Real, too. In that room at the gable a child
Was born while the wind chilled a summer dawn:
Never looked grey mind on a greyer one
Than when the child's cry broke above the groans.'
'I hope they were both spared.' 'They were. Oh yes.
But flint and clay and childbirth were too real
For this cloud-castle. I had forgot the wind.
Pray do not let me get on to the wind.
You would not understand about the wind.
It is my subject, and compared with me
Those who have always lived on the firm ground
Are quite unreal in this matter of the wind.
There were whole days and nights when the wind and I
Between us shared the world, and the wind ruled

[79]

And I obeyed it and forgot the mist.
My past and the past of the world were in the wind.
Now you will say that though you understand
And feel for me, and so on, you yourself
Would find it different. You are all like that
If once you stand here free from wind and mist:
I might as well be talking to wind and mist.
You would believe the house-agent's young man
Who gives no heed to anything I say.
Good morning. But one word. I want to admit
That I would try the house once more, if I could;
As I should like to try being young again.'

Digging

Today I think
Only with scents, – scents dead leaves yield,
And bracken, and wild carrot's seed,
And the square mustard field;

Odours that rise
When the spade wounds the root of tree,
Rose, currant, raspberry, or goutweed,
Rhubarb or celery;

The smoke's smell, too,
Flowing from where a bonfire burns
The dead, the waste, the dangerous,
And all to sweetness turns.

It is enough
To smell, to crumble the dark earth.
While the robin sings over again
Sad songs of Autumn mirth.

Lob

At hawthorn-time in Wiltshire travelling
In search of something chance would never bring,
An old man's face, by life and weather cut
And coloured, – rough, brown, sweet as any nut, –
A land face, sea-blue-eyed, – hung in my mind
When I had left him many a mile behind.
All he said was: 'Nobody can't stop 'ee. It's
A footpath, right enough. You see those bits
Of mounds – that's where they opened up the barrows
Sixty years since, while I was scaring sparrows.
They thought as there was something to find there,
But couldn't find it, by digging, anywhere.'

To turn back then and seek him, where was the use?
There were three Manningfords, – Abbots, Bohun,
    and Bruce:
And whether Alton, not Manningford, it was,
My memory could not decide, because
There was both Alton Barnes and Alton Priors.
All had their churches, graveyards, farms, and byres,
Lurking to one side up the paths and lanes,
Seldom well seen except by aeroplanes;
And when bells rang, or pigs squealed, or cocks crowed,
Then only heard. Ages ago the road
Approached. The people stood and looked and turned,
Nor asked it to come nearer, nor yet learned
To move out there and dwell in all men's dust.
And yet withal they shot the weathercock, just

Because 'twas he crowed out of tune, they said:
So now the copper weathercock is dead.
If they had reaped their dandelions and sold
Them fairly, they could have afforded gold.

Many years passed, and I went back again
Among those villages, and looked for men
Who might have known my ancient. He himself
Had long been dead or laid upon the shelf,
I thought. One man I asked about him roared
At my description: ''Tis old Bottlesford
He means, Bill.' But another said: 'Of course,
It was Jack Button up at the White Horse.
He's dead, sir, these three years.' This lasted till
A girl proposed Walker of Walker's Hill,
'Old Adam Walker. Adam's Point you'll see
Marked on the maps.'

                'That was her roguery,'
The next man said. He was a squire's son
Who loved wild bird and beast, and dog and gun
For killing them. He had loved them from his birth,
One with another, as he loved the earth.
'The man may be like Button, or Walker, or
Like Bottlesford, that you want, but far more
He sounds like one I saw when I was a child.
I could almost swear to him. The man was wild
And wandered. His home was where he was free.
Everybody has met one such man as he.
Does he keep clear old paths that no one uses
But once a life-time when he loves or muses?
He is English as this gate, these flowers, this mire.
And when at eight years old Lob-lie-by-the-fire

Came in my books, this was the man I saw.
He has been in England as long as dove and daw,
Calling the wild cherry tree the merry tree,
The rose campion Bridget-in-her-bravery;
And in a tender mood he, as I guess,
Christened one flower Love-in-idleness,
And while he walked from Exeter to Leeds
One April called all cuckoo-flowers Milkmaids.
From him old herbal Gerard learnt, as a boy,
To name wild clematis the Traveller's-joy.
Our blackbirds sang no English till his ear
Told him they called his Jan Toy "Pretty dear".
(She was Jan Toy the Lucky, who, having lost
A shilling, and found a penny loaf, rejoiced.)
For reasons of his own to him the wren
Is Jenny Pooter. Before all other men
'Twas he first called the Hog's Back the Hog's Back.
That Mother Dunch's Buttocks should not lack
Their name was his care. He too could explain
Totteridge and Totterdown and Juggler's Lane:
He knows, if anyone. Why Tumbling Bay,
Inland in Kent, is called so, he might say.

'But little he says compared with what he does.
If ever a sage troubles him he will buzz
Like a beehive to conclude the tedious fray:
And the sage, who knows all languages, runs away.
Yet Lob has thirteen hundred names for a fool,
And though he never could spare time for school
To unteach what the fox so well expressed,
On biting the cock's head off, – Quietness is best, –
 He can talk quite as well as anyone
 After his thinking is forgot and done.

He first of all told someone else's wife,
For a farthing she'd skin a flint and spoil a knife
Worth sixpence skinning it. She heard him speak:
"She had a face as long as a wet week"
Said he, telling the tale in after years.
With blue smock and with gold rings in his ears,
Sometimes he is a pedlar, not too poor
To keep his wit. This is tall Tom that bore
The logs in, and with Shakespeare in the hall
Once talked, when icicles hung by the wall.
As Herne the Hunter he has known hard times.
On sleepless nights he made up weather rhymes
Which others spoilt. And, Hob being then his name,
He kept the hog that thought the butcher came
To bring his breakfast. "You thought wrong," said Hob.
When there were kings in Kent this very Lob,
Whose sheep grew fat and he himself grew merry,
Wedded the king's daughter of Canterbury;
For he alone, unlike squire, lord, and king,
Watched a night by her without slumbering;
He kept both waking. When he was but a lad
He won a rich man's heiress, deaf, dumb, and sad,
By rousing her to laugh at him. He carried
His donkey on his back. So they were married.
And while he was a little cobbler's boy
He tricked the giant coming to destroy
Shrewsbury by flood. "And how far is it yet?"
The giant asked in passing. "I forget;
But see these shoes I've worn out on the road
And we're not there yet." He emptied out his load
Of shoes for mending. The giant let fall from his spade
The earth for damming Severn, and thus made
The Wrekin hill; and little Ercall hill

Rose where the giant scraped his boots. While still
So young, our Jack was chief of Gotham's sages.
But long before he could have been wise, ages
Earlier than this, while he grew thick and strong
And ate his bacon, or, at times, sang a song
And merely smelt it, as Jack the giant-killer
He made a name. He too ground up the miller,
The Yorkshireman who ground men's bones for flour.

'Do you believe Jack dead before his hour?
Or that his name is Walker, or Bottlesford,
Or Button, a mere clown, or squire, or lord?
The man you saw, – Lob-lie-by-the-fire, Jack Cade,
Jack Smith, Jack Moon, poor Jack of every trade,
Young Jack, or old Jack, or Jack What-d'ye-call,
Jack-in-the-hedge, or Robin-run-by-the-wall,
Robin Hood, Ragged Robin, lazy Bob,
One of the lords of No Man's Land, good Lob, –
Although he was seen dying at Waterloo,
Hastings, Agincourt, and Sedgemoor too, –
Lives yet. He never will admit he is dead
Till millers cease to grind men's bones for bread,
Not till our weathercock crows once again
And I remove my house out of the lane
On to the road.' With this he disappeared
In hazel and thorn tangled with old-man's-beard.
But one glimpse of his back, as there he stood,
Choosing his way, proved him of old Jack's blood,
Young Jack perhaps, and now a Wiltshireman
As he has oft been since his days began.

Lovers

The two men in the road were taken aback.
The lovers came out shading their eyes from the sun,
And never was white so white, or black so black,
As her cheeks and hair. 'There are more things than one
A man might turn into a wood for, Jack,'
Said George; Jack whispered: 'He has not got a gun.
It's a bit too much of a good thing, I say.
They are going the other road, look. And see her run.' –
She ran – 'What a thing it is, this picking may.'

In Memoriam (Easter, 1915)

The flowers left thick at nightfall in the wood
This Eastertide call into mind the men,
Now far from home, who, with their sweethearts, should
Have gathered them and will do never again.

Head and Bottle

The downs will lose the sun, white alyssum
Lose the bees' hum;
But head and bottle tilted back in the cart
Will never part
Till I am cold as midnight and all my hours
Are beeless flowers.
He neither sees, nor hears, nor smells, nor thinks,
But only drinks,
Quiet in the yard where tree trunks do not lie
More quietly.

Home

Often I had gone this way before:
But now it seemed I never could be
And never had been anywhere else;
'Twas home; one nationality
We had, I and the birds that sang,
One memory.

They welcomed me. I had come back
That eve somehow from somewhere far:
The April mist, the chill, the calm,
Meant the same thing familiar
And pleasant to us, and strange too,
Yet with no bar.

The thrush on the oaktop in the lane
Sang his last song, or last but one;
And as he ended, on the elm
Another had but just begun
His last; they knew no more than I
The day was done.

Then past his dark white cottage front
A labourer went along, his tread
Slow, half with weariness, half with ease;
And, through the silence, from his shed
The sound of sawing rounded all
That silence said.

Health

Four miles at a leap, over the dark hollow land,
To the frosted steep of the down and its junipers
    black,
Travels my eye with equal ease and delight:
And scarce could my body leap four yards.

This is the best and the worst of it –
Never to know,
Yet to imagine gloriously, pure health.

Today, had I suddenly health,
I could not satisfy the desire of my heart
Unless health abated it,
So beautiful is the air in its softness and clearness,
    while Spring
Promises all and fails in nothing as yet;
And what blue and what white is I never knew
Before I saw this sky blessing the land.

For had I health I could not ride or run or fly
So far or so rapidly over the land
As I desire: I should reach Wiltshire tired;
I should have changed my mind before I could be
    in Wales.
I could not love; I could not command love.
Beauty would still be far off
However many hills I climbed over;
Peace would still be farther.

Maybe I should not count it anything
To leap these four miles with the eye;
And either I should not be filled almost to bursting
    with desire,
Or with my power desire would still keep pace.

Yet I am not satisfied
Even with knowing I never could be satisfied.
With health and all the power that lies
In maiden beauty, poet and warrior,
In Caesar, Shakespeare, Alcibiades,
Mazeppa, Leonardo, Michelangelo,
In any maiden whose smile is lovelier
Than sunlight upon dew,
I could not be as the wagtail running up and down
The warm tiles of the roof slope, twittering
Happily and sweetly as if the sun itself
Extracted the song
As the hand makes sparks from the fur of a cat:

I could not be as the sun.
Nor should I be content to be
As little as the bird or as mighty as the sun.
For the bird knows not of the sun,
And the sun regards not the bird.
But I am almost proud to love both bird and sun,
Though scarce this Spring could my body leap
    four yards.

The Chalk Pit

'Is this the road that climbs above and bends
Round what was once a chalk pit: now it is
By accident an amphitheatre.
Some ash trees standing ankle-deep in brier
And bramble act the parts, and neither speak
Nor stir.' 'But see: they have fallen, every one,
And brier and bramble have grown over them.'
'That is the place. As usual no one is here.
Hardly can I imagine the drop of the axe,
And the smack that is like an echo, sounding here.'
'I do not understand.' 'Why, what I mean is
That I have seen the place two or three times
At most, and that its emptiness and silence
And stillness haunt me, as if just before
It was not empty, silent, still, but full
Of life of some kind, perhaps tragical.
Has anything unusual happened here?'
'Not that I know of. It is called the Dell.
They have not dug chalk here for a century.
That was the ash-trees' age. But I will ask.'
'No. Do not. I prefer to make a tale,
Or better leave it like the end of a play,
Actors and audience and lights all gone;
For so it looks now. In my memory
Again and again I see it, strangely dark,
And vacant of a life but just withdrawn.
We have not seen the woodman with the axe.
Some ghost has left it now as we two came.'

'And yet you doubted if this were the road?'
'Well, sometimes I have thought of it and failed
To place it. No. And I am not quite sure,
Even now, this is it. For another place,
Real or painted, may have combined with it.
Or I myself a long way back in time . . .'
'Why, as to that, I used to meet a man –
I had forgotten, – searching for birds' nests
Along the road and in the chalk pit too.
The wren's hole was an eye that looked at him
For recognition. Every nest he knew.
He got a stiff neck, by looking this side or that,
Spring after spring, he told me, with his laugh, –
A sort of laugh. He was a visitor,
A man of forty, – smoked and strolled about.
At orts and crosses Pleasure and Pain had played
On his brown features; – I think both had lost; –
Mild and yet wild too. You may know the kind.
And once or twice a woman shared his walks,
A girl of twenty with a brown boy's face,
And hair brown as a thrush or as a nut,
Thick eyebrows, glinting eyes –' 'You have said enough.
A pair, – free thought, free love, – I know the breed:
I shall not mix my fancies up with them.'
'You please yourself. I should prefer the truth
Or nothing. Here, in fact, is nothing at all
Except a silent place that once rang loud,
And trees and us – imperfect friends, we men
And trees since time began; and nevertheless
Between us still we breed a mystery.'

Fifty Faggots

There they stand, on their ends, the fifty faggots
That once were underwood of hazel and ash
In Jenny Pinks's Copse. Now, by the hedge
Close packed, they make a thicket fancy alone
Can creep through with the mouse and wren.
   Next Spring
A blackbird or a robin will nest there,
Accustomed to them, thinking they will remain
Whatever is for ever to a bird:
This Spring it is too late; the swift has come.
'Twas a hot day for carrying them up:
Better they will never warm me, though they must
Light several Winters' fires. Before they are done
The war will have ended, many other things
Have ended, maybe, that I can no more
Foresee or more control than robin and wren.

I built myself a house of glass

I built myself a house of glass:
It took me years to make it:
And I was proud. But now, alas,
Would God someone would break it.

But it looks too magnificent.
No neighbour casts a stone
From where he dwells, in tenement
Or palace of glass, alone.

Words

Out of us all
That make rhymes,
Will you choose
Sometimes –
As the winds use
A crack in a wall
Or a drain,
Their joy or their pain
To whistle through –
Choose me,
You English words?

I know you:
You are light as dreams,
Tough as oak,
Precious as gold,
As poppies and corn,
Or an old cloak:
Sweet as our birds
To the ear,
As the burnet rose
In the heat
Of Midsummer:
Strange as the races
Of dead and unborn:
Strange and sweet
Equally,
And familiar,
To the eye,

As the dearest faces
That a man knows,
And as lost homes are:
But though older far
Than oldest yew, –
As our hills are, old. –
Worn new
Again and again:
Young as our streams
After rain:
And as dear
As the earth which you prove
That we love.

Make me content
With some sweetness
From Wales
Whose nightingales
Have no wings, –
From Wiltshire and Kent
And Herefordshire,
And the villages there, –
From the names, and the things
No less.

Let me sometimes dance
With you,
Or climb
Or stand perchance
In ecstasy,
Fixed and free
In a rhyme,
As poets do.

The Word

There are so many things I have forgot,
That once were much to me, or that were not,
All lost, as is a childless woman's child
And its child's children, in the undefiled
Abyss of what can never be again.
I have forgot, too, names of the mighty men
That fought and lost or won in the old wars,
Of kings and fiends and gods, and most of the stars.
Some things I have forgot that I forget.
But lesser things there are, remembered yet,
Than all the others. One name that I have not –
Though 'tis an empty thingless name – forgot
Never can die because Spring after Spring
Some thrushes learn to say it as they sing.
There is always one at midday saying it clear
And tart – the name, only the name I hear.
While perhaps I am thinking of the elder scent
That is like food, or while I am content
With the wild rose scent that is like memory,
This name suddenly is cried out to me
From somewhere in the bushes by a bird
Over and over again, a pure thrush word.

Haymaking

After night's thunder far away had rolled
The fiery day had a kernel sweet of cold,
And in the perfect blue the clouds uncurled,
Like the first gods before they made the world
And misery, swimming the stormless sea
In beauty and in divine gaiety.
The smooth white empty road was lightly strewn
With leaves – the holly's Autumn falls in June –
And fir cones standing stiff up in the heat.
The mill-foot water tumbled white and lit
With tossing crystals, happier than any crowd
Of children pouring out of school aloud.
And in the little thickets where a sleeper
For ever might lie lost, the nettle-creeper
And garden warbler sang unceasingly;
While over them shrill shrieked in his fierce glee
The swift with wings and tail as sharp and narrow
As if the bow had flown off with the arrow.
Only the scent of woodbine and hay new-mown
Travelled the road. In the field sloping down,
Park-like, to where its willows showed the brook,
Haymakers rested. The tosser lay forsook
Out in the sun; and the long waggon stood
Without its team, it seemed it never would
Move from the shadow of that single yew.
The team, as still, until their task was due,
Beside the labourers enjoyed the shade
That three squat oaks mid-field together made

Upon a circle of grass and weed uncut,
And on the hollow, once a chalk-pit, but
Now brimmed with nut and elder-flower so clean.
The men leaned on their rakes, about to begin,
But still. And all were silent. All was old,
This morning time, with a great age untold,
Older than Clare and Cobbett, Morland and Crome,
Than, at the field's far edge, the farmer's home,
A white house crouched at the foot of a great tree.
Under the heavens that know not what years be
The men, the beasts, the trees, the implements
Uttered even what they will in times far hence –
All of us gone out of the reach of change –
Immortal in a picture of an old grange.

A Dream

Over known fields with an old friend in dream
I walked, but came sudden to a strange stream.
Its dark waters were bursting out most bright
From a great mountain's heart into the light.
They ran a short course under the sun, then back
Into a pit they plunged, once more as black
As at their birth; and I stood thinking there
How white, had the day shone on them, they were,
Heaving and coiling. So by the roar and hiss
And by the mighty motion of the abyss
I was bemused, that I forgot my friend
And neither saw nor sought him till the end,
When I awoke from waters unto men
Saying: 'I shall be here some day again.'

The Brook

Seated once by a brook, watching a child
Chiefly that paddled, I was thus beguiled.
Mellow the blackbird sang and sharp the thrush
Not far off in the oak and hazel brush,
Unseen. There was a scent like honeycomb
From mugwort dull. And down upon the dome
Of the stone the cart-horse kicks against so oft
A butterfly alighted. From aloft
He took the heat of the sun, and from below.
On the hot stone he perched contented so,
As if never a cart would pass again
That way; as if I were the last of men
And he the first of insects to have earth
And sun together and to know their worth.
I was divided between him and the gleam,
The motion, and the voices, of the stream,
The waters running frizzled over gravel,
That never vanish and for ever travel.
A grey flycatcher silent on a fence
And I sat as if we had been there since
The horseman and the horse lying beneath
The fir-tree-covered barrow on the heath,
The horseman and the horse with silver shoes,
Galloped the downs last. All that I could lose
I lost. And then the child's voice raised the dead.
'No one's been here before' was what she said
And what I felt, yet never should have found
A word for, while I gathered sight and sound.

Aspens

All day and night, save winter, every weather,
Above the inn, the smithy, and the shop,
The aspens at the cross-roads talk together
Of rain, until their last leaves fall from the top.

Out of the blacksmith's cavern comes the ringing
Of hammer, shoe, and anvil; out of the inn
The clink, the hum, the roar, the random singing –
The sounds that for these fifty years have been.

The whisper of the aspens is not drowned,
And over lightless pane and footless road,
Empty as sky, with every other sound
Not ceasing, calls their ghosts from their abode,

A silent smithy, a silent inn, nor fails
In the bare moonlight or the thick-furred gloom,
In tempest or the night of nightingales,
To turn the cross-roads to a ghostly room.

And it would be the same were no house near.
Over all sorts of weather, men, and times,
Aspens must shake their leaves and men may hear
But need not listen, more than to my rhymes.

Whatever wind blows, while they and I have leaves
We cannot other than an aspen be
That ceaselessly, unreasonably grieves,
Or so men think who like a different tree.

The Mill-Water

Only the sound remains
Of the old mill;
Gone is the wheel;
On the prone roof and walls the nettle reigns.

Water that toils no more
Dangles white locks
And, falling, mocks
The music of the mill-wheel's busy roar.

Pretty to see, by day
Its sound is naught
Compared with thought
And talk and noise of labour and of play.

Night makes the difference.
In calm moonlight,
Gloom infinite,
The sound comes surging in upon the sense:

Solitude, company, –
When it is night, –
Grief or delight
By it must haunted or concluded be.

Often the silentness
Has but this one
Companion;
Wherever one creeps in the other is:

Sometimes a thought is drowned
By it, sometimes
Out of it climbs;
All thoughts begin or end upon this sound,

Only the idle foam
Of water falling
Changelessly calling,
Where once men had a work-place and a home.

Cock-Crow

Out of the wood of thoughts that grows by night
To be cut down by the sharp axe of light, –
Out of the night, two cocks together crow,
Cleaving the darkness with a silver blow:
And bright before my eyes twin trumpeters stand,
Heralds of splendour, one at either hand,
Each facing each as in a coat of arms:
The milkers lace their boots up at the farms.

A Private

This ploughman dead in battle slept out of doors
Many a frosty night, and merrily
Answered staid drinkers, good bedmen, and all bores:
'At Mrs Greenland's Hawthorn Bush,' said he,
'I slept.' None knew which bush. Above the town,
Beyond 'The Drover', a hundred spot the down
In Wiltshire. And where now at last he sleeps
More sound in France – that, too, he secret keeps.

This is no case of petty right or wrong

This is no case of petty right or wrong
That politicians or philosophers
Can judge. I hate not Germans, nor grow hot
With love of Englishmen, to please newspapers.
Beside my hate for one fat patriot
My hatred of the Kaiser is love true: –
A kind of god he is, banging a gong.
But I have not to choose between the two,
Or between justice and injustice. Dinned
With war and argument I read no more
Than in the storm smoking along the wind
Athwart the wood. Two witches' cauldrons roar.
From one the weather shall rise clear and gay;
Out of the other an England beautiful
And like her mother that died yesterday.
Little I know or care if, being dull,
I shall miss something that historians
Can rake out of the ashes when perchance
The phoenix broods serene above their ken.
But with the best and meanest Englishmen
I am one in crying, God save England, lest
We lose what never slaves and cattle blessed.
The ages made her that made us from the dust:
She is all we know and live by, and we trust
She is good and must endure, loving her so:
And as we love ourselves we hate her foe.

Rain

Rain, midnight rain, nothing but the wild rain
On this bleak hut, and solitude, and me
Remembering again that I shall die
And neither hear the rain nor give it thanks
For washing me cleaner than I have been
Since I was born into this solitude.
Blessed are the dead that the rain rains upon:
But here I pray that none whom once I loved
Is dying tonight or lying still awake
Solitary, listening to the rain,
Either in pain or thus in sympathy
Helpless among the living and the dead,
Like a cold water among broken reeds,
Myriads of broken reeds all still and stiff,
Like me who have no love which this wild rain
Has not dissolved except the love of death,
If love it be towards what is perfect and
Cannot, the tempest tells me, disappoint.

The clouds that are so light

The clouds that are so light,
Beautiful, swift and bright,
Cast shadows on field and park
Of the earth that is so dark,

And even so now, light one!
Beautiful, swift and bright one!
You let fall on a heart that was dark,
Unillumined, a deeper mark.

But clouds would have, without earth
To shadow, far less worth:
Away from your shadow on me
Your beauty less would be,

And if it still be treasured
An age hence, it shall be measured
By this small dark spot
Without which it were not.

Roads

I love roads:
The goddesses that dwell
Far along invisible
Are my favourite gods.

Roads go on
While we forget, and are
Forgotten like a star
That shoots and is gone.

On this earth 'tis sure
We men have not made
Anything that doth fade
So soon, so long endure:

The hill road wet with rain
In the sun would not gleam
Like a winding stream
If we trod it not again.

They are lonely
While we sleep, lonelier
For lack of the traveller
Who is now a dream only.

From dawn's twilight
And all the clouds like sheep
On the mountains of sleep
They wind into the night.

The next turn may reveal
Heaven: upon the crest
The close pine clump, at rest
And black, may Hell conceal.

Often footsore, never
Yet of the road I weary,
Though long and steep and dreary
As it winds on for ever.

Helen of the roads,
The mountain ways of Wales
And the Mabinogion tales,
Is one of the true gods,

Abiding in the trees,
The threes and fours so wise,
The larger companies,
That by the roadside be,

And beneath the rafter
Else uninhabited
Excepting by the dead;
And it is her laughter

At morn and night I hear
When the thrush cock sings
Bright irrelevant things,
And when the chanticleer

Calls back to their own night
Troops that make loneliness
With their light footsteps' press,
As Helen's own are light.

Now all roads lead to France
And heavy is the tread
Of the living; but the dead
Returning lightly dance:

Whatever the road bring
To me or take from me,
They keep me company
With their pattering,

Crowding the solitude
Of the loops over the downs,
Hushing the roar of towns
And their brief multitude.

February Afternoon

Men heard this roar of parleying starlings, saw,
   A thousand years ago even as now,
   Black rooks with white gulls following the plough
So that the first are last until a caw
Commands that last are first again, – a law
   Which was of old when one, like me, dreamed how
   A thousand years might dust lie on his brow
Yet thus would birds do between hedge and shaw.

Time swims before me, making as a day
   A thousand years, while the broad ploughland oak
   Roars mill-like and men strike and bear the stroke
     Of war as ever, audacious or resigned,
And God still sits aloft in the array
      That we have wrought him, stone-deaf and stone-blind.

I may come near loving you

I may come near loving you
When you are dead
And there is nothing to do
And much to be said.

To repent that day will be
Impossible
For you and vain for me
The truth to tell.

I shall be sorry for
Your impotence:
You can do and undo no more
When you go hence,

Cannot even forgive
The funeral.
But not so long as you live
Can I love you at all.

Those things that poets said

Those things that poets said
Of love seemed true to me
When I loved and I fed
On love and poetry equally.

But now I wish I knew
If theirs were love indeed,
Or if mine were the true
And theirs some other lovely weed:

For certainly not thus,
Then or thereafter, I
Loved ever. Between us
Decide, good Love, before I die.

Only, that once I loved
By this one argument
Is very plainly proved:
I loving not am different.

No one so much as you

No one so much as you
Loves this my clay,
Or would lament as you
Its dying day.

You know me through and through
Though I have not told,
And though with what you know
You are not bold.

None ever was so fair
As I thought you:
Not a word can I bear
Spoken against you.

All that I ever did
For you seemed coarse
Compared with what I hid
Nor put in force.

My eyes scarce dare meet you
Lest they should prove
I but respond to you
And do not love.

We look and understand,
We cannot speak
Except in trifles and
Words the most weak.

For I at most accept
Your love, regretting
That is all: I have kept
Only a fretting

That I could not return
All that you gave
And could not ever burn
With the love you have,

Till sometimes it did seem
Better it were
Never to see you more
Than linger here

With only gratitude
Instead of love –
A pine in solitude
Cradling a dove.

The Unknown

She is most fair,
And when they see her pass
The poets' ladies
Look no more in the glass
But after her.

On a bleak moor
Running under the moon
She lures a poet,
Once proud or happy, soon
Far from his door.

Beside a train,
Because they saw her go,
Or failed to see her,
Travellers and watchers know
Another pain.

The simple lack
Of her is more to me
Than others' presence,
Whether life splendid be
Or utter black.

I have not seen,
I have no news of her;
I can tell only
She is not here, but there
She might have been.

She is to be kissed
Only perhaps by me;
She may be seeking
Me and no other: she
May not exist.

Celandine

Thinking of her had saddened me at first,
Until I saw the sun on the celandines lie
Redoubled, and she stood up like a flame,
A living thing, not what before I nursed,
The shadow I was growing to love almost,
The phantom, not the creature with bright eye
That I had thought never to see, once lost.

She found the celandines of February
Always before us all. Her nature and name
Were like those flowers, and now immediately
For a short swift eternity back she came,
Beautiful, happy, simply as when she wore
Her brightest bloom among the winter hues
Of all the world; and I was happy too,
Seeing the blossoms and the maiden who
Had seen them with me Februarys before,
Bending to them as in and out she trod
And laughed, with locks sweeping the mossy sod.

But this was a dream: the flowers were not true,
Until I stooped to pluck from the grass there
One of five petals and I smelt the juice
Which made me sigh, remembering she was no more,
Gone like a never perfectly recalled air.

'Home'

Fair was the morning, fair our tempers, and
We had seen nothing fairer than that land,
Though strange, and the untrodden snow that made
Wild of the tame, casting out all that was
Not wild and rustic and old; and we were glad.

Fair, too, was afternoon, and first to pass
Were we that league of snow, next the north wind

There was nothing to return for, except need,
And yet we sang nor ever stopped for speed,
As we did often with the start behind.
Faster still strode we when we came in sight
Of the cold roofs where we must spend the night.
Happy we had not been there, nor could be.
Though we had tasted sleep and food and fellowship
Together long.

        'How quick' to someone's lip
The words came, 'will the beaten horse run home.'

The word 'home' raised a smile in us all three,
And one repeated it, smiling just so
That all knew what he meant and none would say.
Between three counties far apart that lay
We were divided and looked strangely each
At the other, and we knew we were not friends
But fellows in a union that ends
With the necessity for it, as it ought.

Never a word was spoken, not a thought
Was thought, of what the look meant with the word
'Home' as we walked and watched the sunset blurred.
And then to me the word, only the word,
'Homesick', as it were playfully occurred:
No more.

        If I should ever more admit
Than the mere word I could not endure it
For a day longer: this captivity
Must somehow come to an end, else I should be
Another man, as often now I seem,
Or this life be only an evil dream.

Thaw

Over the land freckled with snow half-thawed
The speculating rooks at their nests cawed
And saw from elm-tops, delicate as flower of grass,
What we below could not see, Winter pass.

If I should ever by chance

If I should ever by chance grow rich
I'll buy Codham, Cockridden, and Childerditch,
Roses, Pyrgo, and Lapwater,
And let them all to my elder daughter.
The rent I shall ask of her will be only
Each year's first violets, white and lonely,
The first primroses and orchises –
She must find them before I do, that is.
But if she finds a blossom on furze
Without rent they shall all for ever be hers,
Whenever I am sufficiently rich:
Codham, Cockridden, and Childerditch,
Roses, Pyrgo and Lapwater, –
I shall give them all to my elder daughter.

If I were to own

If I were to own this countryside
As far as a man in a day could ride,
And the Tyes were mine for giving or letting, –
Wingle Tye and Margaretting
Tye, – and Skreens, Gooshays, and Cockerells,
Shellow, Rochetts, Bandish, and Pickerells,
Martins, Lambkins, and Lillyputs,
Their copses, ponds, roads, and ruts,
Fields where plough-horses steam and plovers
Fling and whimper, hedges that lovers
Love, and orchards, shrubberies, walls
Where the sun untroubled by north wind falls,
And single trees where the thrush sings well
His proverbs untranslatable,
I would give them all to my son
If he would let me any one
For a song, a blackbird's song, at dawn.
He should have no more, till on my lawn
Never a one was left, because I
Had shot them to put them into a pie, –
His Essex blackbirds, every one,
And I was left old and alone.

Then unless I could pay, for rent, a song
As sweet as a blackbird's, and as long –
No more – he should have the house, not I:
Margaretting or Wingle Tye,

Or it might be Skreens, Gooshays, or Cockerells,
Shellow, Rochetts, Bandish, or Pickerells,
Martins, Lambkins, or Lillyputs,
Should be his till the cart tracks had no ruts.

What shall I give?

What shall I give my daughter the younger
More than will keep her from cold and hunger?
I shall not give her anything.
If she shared South Weald and Havering,
Their acres, the two brooks running between,
Paine's Brook and Weald Brook,
With pewit, woodpecker, swan, and rook,
She would be no richer than the queen
Who once on a time sat in Havering Bower
Alone, with the shadows, pleasure and power.
She could do no more with Samarcand,
Or the mountains of a mountain land
And its far white house above cottages
Like Venus above the Pleiades.
Her small hands I would not cumber
With so many acres and their lumber,
But leave her Steep and her own world
And her spectacled self with hair uncurled,
Wanting a thousand little things
That time without contentment brings.

And you, Helen

And you, Helen, what should I give you?
So many things I would give you
Had I an infinite great store
Offered me and I stood before
To choose. I would give you youth,
All kinds of loveliness and truth,
A clear eye as good as mine,
Lands, waters, flowers, wine,
As many children as your heart
Might wish for, a far better art
Than mine can be, all you have lost
Upon the travelling waters tossed,
Or given to me. If I could choose
Freely in that great treasure-house
Anything from any shelf,
I would give you back yourself,
And power to discriminate
What you want and want it not too late,
Many fair days free from care
And heart to enjoy both foul and fair,
And myself, too, if I could find
Where it lay hidden and it proved kind.

Like the touch of rain

Like the touch of rain she was
On a man's flesh and hair and eyes
When the joy of walking thus
Has taken him by surprise:

With the love of the storm he burns,
He sings, he laughs, well I know how,
But forgets when he returns
As I shall not forget her 'Go now.'

Those two words shut a door
Between me and the blessed rain
That was never shut before
And will not open again.

When we two walked

When we two walked in Lent
We imagined that happiness
Was something different
And this was something less.

But happy were we to hide
Our happiness, not as they were
Who acted in their pride
Juno and Jupiter:

For the Gods in their jealousy
Murdered that wife and man,
And we that were wise live free
To recall our happiness then.

Tall Nettles

Tall nettles cover up, as they have done
These many springs, the rusty harrow, the plough
Long worn out, and the roller made of stone:
Only the elm butt tops the nettles now.

This corner of the farmyard I like most:
As well as any bloom upon a flower
I like the dust on the nettles, never lost
Except to prove the sweetness of a shower.

The Watchers

By the ford at the town's edge
Horse and carter rest:
The carter smokes on the bridge
Watching the water press in swathes
    about his horse's chest.

From the inn one watches, too,
In the room for visitors
That has no fire, but a view
And many cases of stuffed fish, vermin,
    and kingfishers.

The Cherry Trees

The cherry trees bend over and are shedding
On the old road where all that passed are dead,
Their petals, strewing the grass as for a wedding
This early May morn when there is none to wed.

It rains

It rains, and nothing stirs within the fence
Anywhere through the orchard's untrodden, dense
Forest of parsley. The great diamonds
Of rain on the grassblades there is none to break,
Or the fallen petals further down to shake.

And I am nearly as happy as possible
To search the wilderness in vain though well,
To think of two walking, kissing there,
Drenched, yet forgetting the kisses of the rain:
Sad, too, to think that never, never again,

Unless alone, so happy shall I walk
In the rain. When I turn away, on its fine stalk
Twilight has fined to naught, the parsley flower
Figures, suspended still and ghostly white,
The past hovering as it revisits the light.

Some eyes condemn

Some eyes condemn the earth they gaze upon:
Some wait patiently till they know far more
Than earth can tell them: some laugh at the whole
As folly of another's making: one
I knew that laughed because he saw, from core
To rind, not one thing worth the laugh his soul
Had ready at waking: some eyes have begun
With laughing; some stand startled at the door.

Others, too, I have seen rest, question, roll,
Dance, shoot. And many I have loved watching. Some
I could not take my eyes from till they turned
And loving died. I had not found my goal.
But thinking of your eyes, dear, I become
Dumb: for they flamed, and it was me they burned.

The sun used to shine

The sun used to shine while we two walked
Slowly together, paused and started
Again, and sometimes mused, sometimes talked
As either pleased, and cheerfully parted

Each night. We never disagreed
Which gate to rest on. The to be
And the late past we gave small heed.
We turned from men or poetry

To rumours of the war remote
Only till both stood disinclined
For aught but the yellow flavorous coat
Of an apple wasps had undermined;

Or a sentry of dark betonies,
The stateliest of small flowers on earth,
At the forest verge; or crocuses
Pale purple as if they had their birth

In sunless Hades fields. The war
Came back to mind with the moonrise
Which soldiers in the east afar
Beheld then. Nevertheless, our eyes

Could as well imagine the Crusades
Or Caesar's battles. Everything
To faintness like those rumours fades –
Like the brook's water glittering

Under the moonlight – like those walks
Now – like us two that took them, and
The fallen apples, all the talks
And silences – like memory's sand

When the tide covers it late or soon,
And other men through other flowers
In those fields under the same moon
Go talking and have easy hours.

No one cares less than I

'No one cares less than I,
Nobody knows but God,
Whether I am destined to lie
Under a foreign clod,'
Were the words I made to the bugle call
   in the morning.

But laughing, storming, scorning,
Only the bugles know
What the bugles say in the morning,
And they do not care, when they blow
The call that I heard and made words to
   early this morning.

As the team's head-brass

As the team's head-brass flashed out on the turn
The lovers disappeared into the wood.
I sat among the boughs of the fallen elm
That strewed an angle of the fallow, and
Watched the plough narrowing a yellow square
Of charlock. Every time the horses turned
Instead of treading me down, the ploughman leaned
Upon the handles to say or ask a word,
About the weather, next about the war.
Scraping the share he faced towards the wood,
And screwed along the furrow till the brass flashed
Once more.
        The blizzard felled the elm whose crest
I sat in, by a woodpecker's round hole,
The ploughman said. 'When will they take it away?'
'When the war's over.' So the talk began –
One minute and an interval of ten,
A minute more and the same interval.
'Have you been out?' 'No.' 'And don't want to, perhaps?'
'If I could only come back again, I should.
I could spare an arm. I shouldn't want to lose
A leg. If I should lose my head, why, so,
I should want nothing more. . . . Have many gone
From here?' 'Yes.' 'Many lost?' 'Yes: a good few.
Only two teams work on the farm this year.
One of my mates is dead. The second day
In France they killed him. It was back in March,
The very night of the blizzard, too. Now if

[141]

He had stayed here we should have moved the tree.'
'And I should not have sat here. Everything
Would have been different. For it would have been
Another world.' 'Ay, and a better, though
If we could see all all might seem good.' Then
The lovers came out of the wood again:
The horses started and for the last time
I watched the clods crumble and topple over
After the ploughshare and the stumbling team.

After you speak

After you speak
And what you meant
Is plain,
My eyes
Meet yours that mean –
With your cheeks and hair –
Something more wise,
More dark,
And far different.
Even so the lark
Loves dust
And nestles in it
The minute
Before he must
Soar in lone flight
So far,
Like a black star
He seems –
A mote
Of singing dust
Afloat
Above,
That dreams
And sheds no light.
I know your lust
Is love.

The Green Roads

The green roads that end in the forest
Are strewn with white goose feathers this June,

Like marks left behind by someone gone to the forest
To show his track. But he has never come back.

Down each green road a cottage looks at the forest.
Round one the nettle towers; two are bathed in flowers.

An old man along the green road to the forest
Strays from one, from another a child alone.

In the thicket bordering the forest,
All day long a thrush twiddles his song.

It is old, but the trees are young in the forest,
All but one like a castle keep, in the middle deep.

That oak saw the ages pass in the forest:
They were a host, but their memories are lost,

For the tree is dead: all things forget the forest
Excepting perhaps me, when now I see

The old man, the child, the goose feathers at the edge
    of the forest,
And hear all day long the thrush repeat his song.

The Gallows

There was a weasel lived in the sun
With all his family,
Till a keeper shot him with his gun
And hung him up on a tree,
Where he swings in the wind and rain,
In the sun and in the snow,
Without pleasure, without pain,
On the dead oak tree bough.

There was a crow who was no sleeper,
But a thief and a murderer
Till a very late hour; and this keeper
Made him one of the things that were,
To hang and flap in rain and wind,
In the sun and in the snow.
There are no more sins to be sinned
On the dead oak tree bough.

There was a magpie, too,
Had a long tongue and a long tail;
He could both talk and do –
But what did that avail?
He, too, flaps in the wind and rain
Alongside weasel and crow,
Without pleasure, without pain,
On the dead oak tree bough.

And many other beasts
And birds, skin, bone and feather,
Have been taken from their feasts
And hung up there together,
To swing and have endless leisure
In the sun and in the snow,
Without pain, without pleasure,
On the dead oak tree bough.

Gone, gone again

Gone, gone again,
May, June, July,
And August gone,
Again gone by,

Not memorable
Save that I saw them go,
As past the empty quays
The rivers flow.

And now again,
In the harvest rain,
The Blenheim oranges
Fall grubby from the trees,

As when I was young –
And when the lost one was here –
And when the war began
To turn young men to dung.

Look at the old house,
Outmoded, dignified,
Dark and untenanted,
With grass growing instead

Of the footsteps of life,
The friendliness, the strife;
In its beds have lain
Youth, love, age and pain:

I am something like that;
Only I am not dead,
Still breathing and interested
In the house that is not dark: –

I am something like that:
Not one pane to reflect the sun,
For the schoolboys to throw at –
They have broken every one.

That girl's clear eyes

That girl's clear eyes utterly concealed all
Except that there was something to reveal.
And what did mine say in the interval?
No more: no less. They are but as a seal
Not to be broken till after I am dead;
And then vainly. Every one of us
This morning at our tasks left nothing said,
In spite of many words. We were sealed thus,
Like tombs. Nor until now could I admit
That all I cared for was the pleasure and pain
I tasted in the stony square sunlit,
Or the dark cloisters, or shade of airy plane,
While music blazed and children, line after line,
Marched past, hiding the 'SEVENTEEN THIRTY-NINE'.

What will they do?

What will they do when I am gone? It is plain
That they will do without me as the rain
Can do without the flowers and the grass
That profit by it and must perish without.
I have but seen them in the loud street pass;
And I was naught to them. I turned about
To see them disappearing carelessly.
But what if I in them as they in me
Nourished what has great value and no price?
Almost I thought that rain thirsts for a draught
Which only in the blossom's chalice lies,
Until that one turned back and lightly laughed.

The Trumpet

Rise up, rise up,
And, as the trumpet blowing
Chases the dreams of men,
As the dawn glowing
The stars that left unlit
The land and water,
Rise up and scatter
The dew that covers
The print of last night's lovers –
Scatter it, scatter it!

While you are listening
To the clear horn,
Forget, men, everything
On this earth newborn,
Except that it is lovelier
Than any mysteries.
Open your eyes to the air
That has washed the eyes of the stars
Through all the dewy night:
Up with the light,
To the old wars;
Arise, arise!

When first

When first I came here I had hope,
Hope for I knew not what. Fast beat
My heart at sight of the tall slope
Or grass and yews, as if my feet

Only by scaling its steps of chalk
Would see something no other hill
Ever disclosed. And now I walk
Down it the last time. Never will

My heart beat so again at sight
Of any hill although as fair
And loftier. For infinite
The change, late unperceived, this year,

The twelfth, suddenly, shows me plain.
Hope now, – not health, nor cheerfulness,
Since they can come and go again,
As often one brief hour witnesses, –

Just hope has gone for ever. Perhaps
I may love other hills yet more
Than this: the future and the maps
Hide something I was waiting for.

One thing I know, that love with chance
And use and time and necessity
Will grow, and louder the heart's dance
At parting than at meeting be.

The Child in the Orchard

'He rolls in the orchard: he is stained with moss
And with earth, the solitary old white horse.
Where is his father and where is his mother
Among all the brown horses? Has he a brother?
I know the swallow, the hawk, and the hern;
But there are two million things for me to learn.

'Who was the lady that rode the white horse
With rings and bells to Banbury Cross?
Was there no other lady in England beside
That a nursery rhyme could take for a ride?
The swift, the swallow, the hawk, and the hern.
There are two million things for me to learn.

'Was there a man once who straddled across
The back of the Westbury White Horse
Over there on Salisbury Plain's green wall?
Was he bound for Westbury, or had he a fall?
The swift, the swallow, the hawk, and the hern.
There are two million things for me to learn.

'Out of all the white horses I know three,
At the age of six; and it seems to me
There is so much to learn, for men,
That I dare not go to bed again.
The swift, the swallow, the hawk, and the hern.
There are millions of things for me to learn.'

Lights Out

I have come to the borders of sleep,
The unfathomable deep
Forest where all must lose
Their way, however straight,
Or winding, soon or late;
They cannot choose.

Many a road and track
That, since the dawn's first crack,
Up to the forest brink,
Deceived the travellers
Suddenly now blurs,
And in they sink.

Here love ends,
Despair, ambition ends,
All pleasure and all trouble,
Although most sweet or bitter,
Here ends in sleep that is sweeter
Than tasks most noble.

There is not any book
Or face of dearest look
That I would not turn from now
To go into the unknown
I must enter and leave alone
I know not how.

The tall forest towers;
Its cloudy foliage lowers
Ahead, shelf above shelf;
Its silence I hear and obey
That I may lose my way
And myself.

The long small room

The long small room that showed willows in the west
Narrowed up to the end the fireplace filled,
Although not wide. I liked it. No one guessed
What need or accident made them so build.

Only the moon, the mouse and the sparrow peeped
In from the ivy round the casement thick.
Of all they saw and heard there they shall keep
The tale for the old ivy and older brick.

When I look back I am like moon, sparrow and mouse
That witnessed what they could never understand
Or alter or prevent in the dark house.
One thing remains the same – this my right hand

Crawling crab-like over the clean white page,
Resting awhile each morning on the pillow,
Then once more starting to crawl on towards age.
The hundred last leaves stream upon the willow.

The Lane

Some day, I think, there will be people enough
In Froxfield to pick all the blackberries
Out of the hedges of Green Lane, the straight
Broad lane where now September hides herself
In bracken and blackberry, harebell and dwarf gorse.
Today, where yesterday a hundred sheep
Were nibbling, halcyon bells shake to the sway
Of waters that no vessel ever sailed . . .
It is a kind of spring: the chaffinch tries
His song. For heat it is like summer too.
This might be winter's quiet. While the glint
Of hollies dark in the swollen hedges lasts –
One mile – and those bells ring, little I know
Or heed if time be still the same, until
The lane ends and once more all is the same.

Out in the dark

Out in the dark over the snow
The fallow fawns invisible go
With the fallow doe;
And the winds blow
Fast as the stars are slow.

Stealthily the dark haunts round
And, when a lamp goes, without sound
At a swifter bound
Than the swiftest hound,
Arrives, and all else is drowned;

And I and star and wind and deer,
Are in the dark together, – near,
Yet far, – and fear
Drums on my ear
In that sage company drear.

How weak and little is the light,
All the universe of sight,
Love and delight,
Before the might,
If you love it not, of night.

from
War Diary

Between 1 January and 8 April 1917, Edward Thomas kept a private diary, the existence of which was not widely known of until its re-emergence in 1970 and publication shortly after. Its pages are heavily creased from either the shell blast on 8 April that knocked him over or that of the following morning, Easter Monday, which killed him.

January 30 Arrived Havre 4 a.m. Light of stars and windows of tall pale houses and electric arcs on quay. March through bales of cotton in sun to camp. The snow first emptying its castor of finest white. Tents. Mess full of subalterns censoring letters. Breakfast at 9.45 a.m. on arrival. Afternoon in Havre, wh[ich] Thorburn likes because it is French. Mess unendurably hot and stuffy, tent unendurably cold till I got into my blankets. Slept well in fug. Snow at night.

February 4 Cold and bright again. Took the section sliding, then work on guns. At 11 came warning to move at 5.30. Packing. Censoring. New servant – Taylor – asked if he had done anything of the kind before, said 'I've a wife and family and I know what comforts are.' Started at 4.45 for station w[ith] guns – held up 1½ hours by train across road – 2 hours at station doing nothing, 1½ hours entraining guns – platform all cotton bales and men singing 'The nightingales are singing in the pale moonlight (There's a long long trail awinding)'[.] Sgt Major did practically all the work. The long waiting before train starts – men quite silent after first comic cries of 'All tickets' and imitating cattle (35 men in each cattle truck: we have a compartment to 2 officers). As we start at 11 suddenly the silent men all yell 'Hurray' but are silent before we are clear of long desolate platform of cotton and trampled snow and electric light.

February 8 Weather as before. Physical drill, a hasty Welsh Rabbit with honey, and then off in lorries through Alaincourt, Barly, Fosseux, to Berneville – men billet in huge barn of a big uneven farmyard surrounded by spread arched stone barns and bdgs [buildings] with old pump at one side, kitchen at upper end. We forage. Enemy plane like pale moth beautiful among shrapnel bursts. A fine ride over high open snowy country with some woods. Rigging up table in mess and borrowing crockery. The battery is to split for the present: Rubin has taken guns to Saulty, we are for Dainville. A scramble dinner of half cold stuff, mostly standing. Taylor makes a table and says 'Very good, Sir' and 'It[']s the same for all. You gentlemen have to put up with same as us.' Bed early. Rubin returns late. Heavy firing at night. Restless.

February 14 A bad night but feeling better. All day with Horton, and then Horton and Smith, examining O.P.> [Observation Posts] above Agny and Wailly, and then between Achicourt and Beaurains. Fine sunny day – snow melting. Black-headed buntings talk, rooks caw, lovely white puffs of shrapnel round planes high up. Right section does aeroplane shoot in afternoon. Dead campion umbels, and grass rustling on my helmet through trenches. Pretty little copse in deep hollow high up between Ficheux and Dainville, where guns look over to Berneville and Warlus.

February 15 W[ith] Captain observing for a B[attery] T[raining] shoot on Ficheux Mill and edge of Blairville Wood. Fine sun but cold in trench. W working p[ar]ty in after[noon]. Letters arrived at 6. We sorted them and then spent an hour silently reading. 750 letters for men: 17 for me – from Helen, the children, Father, Mother, Eleanor, Freeman, Mrs Freeman, Guthrie, Vernon and Haines. Ev[enin]g reading and writing letters. A quiet evening indoors and out. Taylor says as he mends the fire, 'Well, we have to put up with many discomforts. We are all alike, Sir, all human.' A still starry night with only machine guns and rifles. Slept badly again, and then suddenly with no notice got up from breakfast on the *16th* to do f/c [fire control] on aeroplane shoot (only 10 rounds, observation being bad). Dull day. Left Thorburn on guns at 11.30. Bad temper. After[noon?] up to O.P. but too hazy to observe. A mad Captain with several men driving partridges over the open and whistling and crying 'Mark over'. Kestrels in pairs. Four or five planes hovering and wheeling as kestrels used to over Mutton and Ludcombe. Women hanging clothes to dry on barbed entanglement across the road. Rain at last at 4.15. This morning the old Frenchman living in this ruin burst into our room while we were dressing to complain of our dirt and depredation, and when Rubin was rude in English said he was a Frenchman and had been an officer. Nobody felt the slightest sympathy with his ravings, more than with the old white horse who works a mill walking up and up treadmill.

February 23 Chaffinch sang once. Another dull cold day. Inspected stables, checked inventory of new billet for men in Rue Jeanne d'Arc, went with Colonel round 244, 141 and 234 [battery] positions and O.P. in Achicourt.

After[noon] maps. Partridges twanging in fields. Flooded fields by stream between the 2 sides of Achicourt. Ruined church, churchyard and railway. Sordid ruin of Estaminet with carpenter's shop over it in Rue Jeanne d'Arc – wet, mortar, litter, almanacs, bottles, broken glass, damp beds, dirty paper, knife, crucifix, statuette, old chairs. Our cat moves with the Group wherever it goes, but inspects new house inside and out, windows, fireplaces etc. Paid the Pool gunners (scrapings from several batteries doing odd jobs here). 2 owls in garden at 6. The shelling must have slaughtered many jackdaws but has made home for many more. Finished Frost's 'Mountain Interval'. Wrote to Frost. A quiet still evening. Rubin brought over letters from Helen and Oscar.

February 24 Why do Huns not retaliate on Arras guns? Some day this will be one of the hottest places this side of Hell, if it is this side. Nothing to do here today. Clearer, but still dull and cold with more breeze. Gas Alert off. Wrote to Father. Lushington calls and goes out with Colonel ——. Dined with 244 and Major Berrington and Capt. Angus – a dull long meal with maraschino chocolates at end, Benedictine, whisky and coffee, after soup, hors d'oeuvres, tinned turkey, roast mutton, Xmas pudding, apricots and cream. Gramophone but no fun. Walked back to Arras in dark w Thorburn, challenged by only 2 sentries who were content with 'Friend' tho[ugh] they c[oul]d not see a yard among the ruins. Owls on Daneville r[oa]d. Machine guns and hanging lights above No Man's Land. Cassells and Colonel alone up when I returned at 11. New moon – *last* as I walked from Hatch to Codford.

February 25 A dull m[ornin]g turns sunny and warm. Chaffinches and partridges, moles working on surface.

Beautiful 18th century citadel with church ruined in middle of great barrack square. Huge bastions with sycamores in moat and tangled grass. Walked over citadel to new position with Colonel. Talked to Horton in our orchard. Wrote to Oscar. Artillery lively in the clear sunny noon. I got hot and spring-languid walking up at 4.30 to 244. Gramophone here played 'Anitra's Dance', 'Death of Troll' etc. and 'Allanwater'. Does a mole ever get hit by a shell?

February 26 A clear mg. 8.15–9.30 a.m. incessant field gun firing – raid – German prisoners back at 10.15. Sunshine in white ruins and white squares with Scots standing about. A few shells arrive in Arras, but nobody looked as if anything were happening. While our guns were firing we could not hear one another speak. After[noon] to Achicourt to see if a gun position was visible to Huns – shells and machine gun bullets came over. An 18 pdr [pounder] on a fp [fire point] fired when I was 3 yds off (in front). Fitting aeroplane photos together. Paid out. A sunny day, but cold in this house. Wrote to G. Bottomley. Gramophone. Talk with Berrington and Colonel.

February 27 Fine but chilly. 2 English planes fell, one on fire, as I walked up to 244 in after[noon]: machine gun bullets cut telephone wire close by. Letters from Helen and Irene. Nothing to do but go and see about a billet of 244's collared by an[othe]r B[atter]y. Tea at 244 after seeing 2 of our planes down, one on fire with both burnt to death after alighting. Letters from Helen, Irene and Eleanor.

March 4 Cold but bright clear and breezy. Nothing to do all morning but trace a map and its contours. Col. and I went down to 244 before lunch to see the shell holes of last night and this morning. Hun planes over. More shells came in the after[noon]. The fire is warm but the room cold. Tea with Lushington and Thorburn. Shelling at 5.30 – I don't like it. I wonder where I shall be hit as in bed I wonder if it is better to be on the window or outer side of room or on the chimney on inner side, whether better to be upstairs where you may fall or on the ground floor where you may be worse crushed. Birthday parcels from home.

March 11 Out at 8.30 to Ronville O.P. and studied the ground from Beaurains N. Larks singing over No Man's Land – trench mortars. We were bombarding their front line: they were shooting at Arras. R.F.A. [Royal Field Artillery] officer with me who was quite concerned till he spotted a certain familiar Hun sentry in front line. A clear cloudy day, mild and breezy. 8th shell carrying into Arras. Later Ronville heavily shelled and we retired to dugout. At 6.15 all quiet and heard blackbirds chinking. Scene peaceful, desolate like Dunwich moors except sprinkling of white chalk on the rough brown ground. Lines broken and linesmen out from 2.30 to 7 p.m. A little raid in the night [. . .]

March 14 Ronville O.P. Looking out towards No Man's Land what I thought first was a piece of burnt paper or something turned out to be a bat shaken at last by shells from one of the last sheds in Ronville. A dull cold mg, with some shelling of Arras and St Sauveur and just 3 for us. Talking to Birt and Randall about Glostershire and Wiltshire, particularly Painswick and Marlborough. A still evg – blackbirds singing far off – a spatter of our machine guns – the spit of one enemy bullet – a little rain – no wind – only far off artillery.

March 15 Huns strafe I sector at 5.30. We reply and they

retaliate on Arras and Ronville. Only tired 77s reach O.P. A sunny breezy morning. Tried to climb Arras chimney to observe, but funked. 4 shells nearly got me while I was going and coming. A rotten day. No letters for 5 days.

March 16 Larks and great tits. Ploughing field next to orchard in mist horses and man go right up to crest in view of Hun at Beaurains. Cold and dull. Letters to Helen and Janet. In the battery for the day. Fired 100 rounds from 12–1.30. Sun shining but misty still. Letter from Bronwen. The first thrush I have heard in France sang as I returned to Mess at 6 p.m. Parcel from Mother – my old Artist boots. Wrote to Hodson. A horrible night of bombardment, and the only time I slept I dreamt I was at home and couldn't stay to tea.

March 20 Stiff deep mud all the way up and shelled as we started. Telegraph Hill as quiet as if only rabbits lived there. I took revolver and left this diary behind in case. For it is very exposed and only a few Cornwalls and MGC [Machine Gun Corps] about. But Hun shelled chiefly over our heads into Beaurains all night – like starlings returning 20 or 30 a minute. Horrible flap of 5.9 a little along the trench. Rain and mud and I've to stay till I am relieved tomorrow. Had not brought warm clothes or enough food and had no shelter, nor had telephonists. Shelled all night. But the M.G.C. boy gave me tea. I've no bed. I leant against wall of trench. I got up and looked over. I stamped up and down. I tried to see patrol out. Very light – the only sign of Hun on Telegraph Hill, tho 2 appeared and were sniped at. A terribly long night and cold. Not relieved till 8. Telephonists out repairing line since 4 on the morning of the 21st.

March 31 Up at 5 worn out and wretched. 5.9s flopping on Achicourt while I dressed. Up to Beaurains. There is a chalk-stone cellar with a dripping Bosh dug-out far under and by the last layer of stones is the lilac bush, rather short. Nearby a graveyard for the 'tapferer franzos soldat' [brave French soldiers] with crosses and Hun names. Blackbirds in the clear cold bright morning early in black Beaurains. Sparrows in the elder of the hedge I observe through – a cherry tree just this side of hedge makes projection in trench with its roots. Beautiful clear evening everything dark and soft round Neuville Vitasse, after the rainbow there and the last shower. Night in lilac-bush cellar of stone like Berryfield. Letter to Helen. Machine gun bullets snaking along – hissing like little wormy serpents.

April 1 among the ragged and craggy gables of Beaurains – a beautiful serene clear morning with larks at 5.15 and blackbirds at 6 till it snowed or rained at 8. All day sat writing letters to Helen, Father and Mother by the fire and censoring men's letters etc., an idle day – I could not sleep till I went to bed at 10. Letters from Helen, Baba and Deacon. A fine bright day with showers.

April 5 A dull morning turns misty with rain. Some 4.2s coming over at 10. Air flapping all night as with great sails in strong gusty wind (with artillery) – thick misty windless air. Sods on F/C's [Forward Command's] dug-out begin to be fledged with fine green feathers of yarrow – yarrow. Sun and wind drying the mud. Firing all day, practising barrage etc. Beautiful pale hazy moonlight and the sag and flap of air. Letters to Mother and Helen. HAMLET.

April 6 A lazy morning, being a half day: warm and breezy, with sun and cloud but turned wet. Billets shelled by 4.2:

60 pdrs. hit. In car with Horton to Fosseux and Avesnes and met infantry with yellow patches behind marching soaked up to line – band and pipes at Wanquetin to greet them, playing 'They wind up the Watch on the Rhine' (as Horton calls it). After the shelling Horton remarks: 'The Bosh is a damned good man, isn't he, a damned smart man, you must admit.' Roads worse than ever – no crust left on side roads. Letters from Helen, Mervyn, Mother, Eleanor.

April 7 Up at 6 to O.P. A cold bright day of continuous shelling N. Vitasse and Telegraph Hill. Infantry all over the place in open preparing Prussian Way with boards for wounded. Hardly any shells into Beaurains. Larks, partridges, hedge-sparrows, and magpies by O.P. A great burst in red brick building in N. Vitasse stood up like a birch tree or a fountain. Back at 7.30 in peace. Then at 8.30 a continuous roar of artillery.

April 8 A bright warm Easter day but Achicourt shelled at 12.30 and then at 2.15 so that we all retired to cellar. I had to go over to battery at 3 for a practice barrage, skirting the danger zone, but we were twice interrupted. A 5.9 fell 2 yds from me as I stood by the F/C post. One burst down the back of the office and a piece of dust scratched my neck. No firing from 2–4. Rubin left for a course.

*

The final pages of the diary contain a draft of a poem:

The sorrow of true love is a great sorrow
And true love parting blackens a bright morrow:
Yet almost they equal joys, since their despair
Is but hope blinded by its tears, and clear
Above the storm the heavens wait to be seen.
But greater sorrow from less love has been
That can mistake lack of despair for hope
And knows not tempest and the perfect scope
Of summer, but a frozen drizzle perpetual
Of drops that from remorse and pity fall
And cannot ever shine in the sun or thaw,
Removed eternally from the sun's law.

13.1.17

and the following notes:

The light of the new moon and every star

———

And no more singing for the bird

———

I never understood quite what was meant by God.

———

The morning chill and clear hurts my skin while it delights my mind.

———

Neuville in early morning with its flat straight crest with trees and houses (see Diary April 1) – the beauty of this silent empty scene of no inhabitants and hid troops, but don't know why I could have cried and didn't

Notes

Place and date of composition are noted below, as is place of first magazine and book publication and the version of the text included here; where the first publication and the text are the same only the text is listed.

THIS IS THE CONSTELLATION OF THE LYRE (xv): place and date of composition unknown, but supporting evidence make composition between 1914–15 likely. The poem was discovered by the poet's daughter, Bronwen, shortly before her death in 1975 and passed to her sister Myfanwy for safe keeping: it had been detached by Bronwen from an autograph album, mounted on a scrap of paper and kept in a notebook, thought to be from 1915. Thomas inked stars into the heavy white paper in the shape of the constellation and signed it 'E. T.', which may date it to a time before he adopted his pseudonym 'Edward Eastaway' in February 1915; however, a poem intended for his family required no such disguise, so the significance of the initials may be minimal. Nonetheless, composition between summer of 1914 (when Thomas may have prepared the poem for a homespun magazine that the Frost children were preparing in Dymock) and the spring of 1915 (when Thomas began sending out his poems to journals) seems plausible. The poem was first published in the *Edward Thomas Fellowship Newsletter*, January 1999, and has not previously been collected.

> This is the constellation of the Lyre:
> Its music cannot ever tire,
> For it is silent. No man need fear it:
> Unless he wants to, he will not hear it.
>
> E. T.

UP IN THE WIND (45): Steep (and possibly Ryton), 3 December 1914 (possibly as early as 16 November 1914); *In Memoriam*, July 1919; text: *Collected Poems* (1920) (with correction of printer's typos). The setting is the White Horse Inn at Froxfield, 'the highest pub in Hampshire'; the pub sign remains absent from the frame at time of writing.

MARCH (49): Steep, 5 December 1914; text: *Last Poems* (1918). Thomas appears to follow Frost's advice to look back 'to the paragraphs here and there in such a book as The Pursuit of Spring' for the content and cadence of his verse (Frost to Harold Roy Brennan, 19 December 1925, *American Literature*, vol. 59, no. 1, March 1987, 117).

OLD MAN (51): Steep, 6 December 1914; *Poetry* (Chicago, February 1917), *An Anthology of New Poetry* (1917), *Last Poems*; text: *An Anthology of New Poetry*. In 1909, Gordon Bottomley gave Thomas a cutting of old man (*Artemisia abrotanum*), which he replanted by the front door of Yew Tree Cottage in Steep when the family moved there in the summer of 1913.

THE SIGNPOST (53): Steep, 7 December 1914; text: *Poems* (1917). With the war four months old, Thomas had yet to determine his course of action in a poem which seems likely to have influenced Frost's 'The Road Not Taken'.

THE OTHER (55): Steep, probably 8–13 December 1914 but possibly as late as 24 December 1914; text: *Last Poems*, which follows the only typescript in existence, sent by Thomas to Frost, and now in Dartmouth College Library; no manuscript survives.

THE MOUNTAIN CHAPEL (59): Steep, mid-December 1914; *Last Poems*; text: Julian Thomas, a typescript once held by the poet's brother, which is preferred here to the text of *Last Poems*, in which lines 31–3 ('And yet somewhere, | Near or far off, there's a man could | Be happy here') seem tonally less consistent than 'somewhere'/'some man' chime of the Julian Thomas typescript and the poem's many other exact or near repetitions.

THE MANOR FARM (61): Steep, 24 December 1914; *This England* (1915); text: *Poems*. The setting is Prior's Dean on the Froxfield plateau, where the Elizabethan manor house stands opposite the Norman church and the yew tree.

AN OLD SONG (62): Steep, 25 December 1914; text: *Last Poems*. A different poem with the same title ('The sun set, the wind fell, the sea') was written on 26 December 1914 and published in *Poems*.

THE COMBE (64): Steep, 30 December 1914; text: *Poems*. Probably, the combe at the foot of Ashford Hanger.

THE NEW YEAR (65): Steep, 1 January 1915; text: *Last Poems*. The manuscript in the British Library (Add. Ms. 44990) omits the final line, indicating that Thomas returned to it at a later date.

SNOW (66): Steep, 7 January 1915; *An Anthology of New Poetry*; text: *An Anthology of New Poetry* and *Last Poems*. Myfanwy, the poet's younger daughter, is the child of the poem.

ADLESTROP (67): Steep, 8 January 1915; *New Statesman*, 28 April 1917; text: *Poems*. On 23 June 1914, Thomas and Helen were en route by train to see Robert Frost in Ledington. 'Then we stopped at Adlestrop, thro[ugh] the willows c[oul]d be heard a chain of blackbirds songs at 12.45 and one thrush and no man seen, only a hiss of engine letting off steam. Stopping outside Campden by banks of long grass willow herb and meadowsweet, extraordinary silence between the two periods of travel – looking out on grey dry stones between metals and the shiny metals and over it all the elms willows and long grass – one man clears his throat – and a greater rustic silence. No house in view[.] Stop only for a minute till signal is up.' (FNB75, Berg Collection, New York Public Library)

OVER THE HILLS (68): Steep, 9 January 1915; text: *Last Poems*. The poem was not titled by Thomas in the only surviving manuscript in the British Library and seems likely to have been christened by Eleanor Farjeon and John Freeman.

MAN AND DOG (69): Steep, 20 January 1915; text: *Last Poems*. A notebook entry from 21 November 1914 records 'Going up Stoner in cold strong N. E. wind but a fine cloudy sky at 3, overtook short stiff oldish man taking short quick strides – carrying flag basket and brolly and old coat [. . .] He had come from Childgrove [*sic*] where he's done two halfdays dock-picking this week: is going to Alton [. . .] comes from Christchurch in the New Forest [. . .] He was thinking about soldiers in France – terrible affair – in cold weather, supposing they would be "marching after the enemy" and surely not lying in trenches this winter weather.' (FNB79, Berg) Thomas left this poem untitled in the British Library manuscript.

BEAUTY (71): Steep, 21 January 1915; *Six Poems* (1916), *An Anthology of New Poetry*, *Last Poems*; text: Julian Thomas, which includes two hand-corrections made by Edward Thomas to the typescript that was used for *An Anthology of New Poetry* and *Last Poems*, suggesting that it may be the author's later (and preferred) version.

FIRST KNOWN WHEN LOST (72): Steep, 11 February 1915; text: *Last Poems*. Written on the morning that the poet's son Mervyn left Steep for America with Robert Frost.

THE OWL (73): Steep, 24 February 1915; text: *Poems*. The decision whether to enlist was obsessing Thomas during the first months of 1915.

THE BRIDGE (74): Steep, 12 March 1915; text: *Poems*.

GOOD-NIGHT (75): Steep, (11? or) 16 March 1915; text: *Last Poems*. The poem's generally accepted date of 16 March derives from the British Library manuscript which Thomas dated retrospectively. However, Thomas marked the word 'verse' in his 1915 diary (National Library of Wales) to record the composition of a poem, and no such entry appears on that date; curiously, he records 'verse' twice on 11 March, one of which referred to 'The Child on the Cliff'; the other remains unknown and may be 'Good-night'.

BUT THESE THINGS ALSO (76): Steep, 18 March 1915; text: *Last Poems*.

THE PATH (77): Steep, 26 March 1915; text: *Poems*. A path descends through Ashford Hanger, connecting the house at Wick Green, Froxfield (where the Thomases lived, 1909–13) with the village of Steep and Bedales School which Mervyn and Bronwen attended.

WIND AND MIST (78): Steep, 1 April 1915; *An Anthology of New Poetry*, *Last Poems*; text: *An Anthology of New Poetry*. One of two poems set in the cold, unloved house at Wick Green, Froxfield; the other being 'The New House', written on 19 March 1915. Thomas kept a study in the garden at Wick Green after he moved the family into a cottage in Steep in 1913.

DIGGING (81): Steep, (3? or) 4 April 1915; text: *Last Poems*. The poem's composition date of 4 April derives from the British Library manuscript, yet Thomas's 1915 diary suggests that he began two poems on 3 April, one of which was 'Lob'; the second, unknown, may have been 'Digging' (NLW). The conventional running order of these two poems is reversed here. The title has no basis in manuscript.

LOB (82): Steep, 3 and 4 April 1915; *Form*, April 1916; text: *Poems*. Thomas's Wiltshire friend David 'Dad' Uzzell was the model for the countryman of this poem.

LOVERS (87): Steep, (4? or) 5 April 1915; *An Anthology of New Poetry*, *Last Poems*; text: *An Anthology of New Poetry*. The British Library manuscript records 5 April as the date of composition, but a diary entry for 4 April reads 'Revising and verse. Walk. verse' (NLW), suggesting that the poem may have been begun on the earlier date.

IN MEMORIAM (EASTER, 1915) (88): Steep, (5? or) 6 April 1915; text: *Poems*. Despite its dating in British Library as 6 April, no diary entry for 'verse' exists on this date and it seems likely that

Thomas wrote the poem on 5 April, Easter Monday, where an entries read 'verse and reading' and 'Walk w[ith] Helen' (NLW). On 6 April, Thomas left for London for five days. Easter 1915 saw the first use of gas in warfare; Thomas would be killed on Easter Monday, 1917.

HEAD AND BOTTLE (89): Steep, 14 April 1915; text: *Poems*.

HOME (90): Steep, 17 April 1915; *Root and Branch*, June 1918; text: *Last Poems*. Written after 'talking and strolling with [W. H.] Davies' in Steep on 12 April, when 'Evening of misty stillness after drizzly day – last thrushes on oaks – then man goes by a dark white cottage front to thatched wood lodge and presently began sawing and birds were all still.' (FNB80, 12 April 1915, Berg)

HEALTH (91): Steep, 18 April 1915; text: *Last Poems*. Even before his association with the doctor Godwin Baynes, Thomas was acutely aware of a link between his physical and mental well-being. The title has no basis in manuscript.

THE CHALK PIT (93): Steep, 8 May 1915; text: *Last Poems*, which is the only source for the final six lines which do not appear in the two surviving manuscripts, British Library and M_I, the first of two notebooks that came into Mervyn's possession. British Library has evidence of a stanza break after line 17 but this is not supported by M_I or by *Last Poems*, which must have been based upon a later typescript (now lost), given the presence of the final six lines. The setting is probably the disused pits at Wheatham Hill, along Old Litten Lane that connected Thomas's house at Wick Green to the pits.

FIFTY FAGGOTS (95): British Museum, 13 May 1915; *New Statesman*, 28 April 1917; text: *Poems*. Thomas sent these lines to Frost (15 May 1915, Dartmouth College) saying they were 'founded on carrying up 50 bunts (short faggots of thin and thick brushwood mixed) and putting them against our hedge,' adding, 'are they north of Boston only?' in deference to Frost's collection of that title.

I BUILT MYSELF A HOUSE OF GLASS (96): Hucclecote, 25 (27?) June 1915; *Last Poems*; text: Julian Thomas, which is identical to *Last Poems* except for the stanza break which was omitted from *Last Poems* in error. A manuscript in the Bodleian Library (Don. d. 28) retrospectively dates composition to 25 June, but Thomas's 1915 diary reveals he was travelling that day and the next mention of 'verse' appears on 27 June (NLW). In his memoir of *Childhood* (43) he writes, 'I discovered the joy of throwing stones over into the unknown depths of a great garden and hearing the glass-house break.' The title has no basis in manuscript.

WORDS (97): 'Hucclecote and on the road from Gloster to Coventry', 26–8 June 1915, *Form*, April 1916; text: *Poems*. On 26 May, Thomas retraced his 1914 walk with Robert Frost up May Hill. Diary records entries for 'verse' on 27 and 28 June (NLW).

THE WORD (99): 'Steep again', 5 July 1915; *Poetry* (Chicago, February 1917), *An Anthology of New Poetry*; text: *An Anthology of New Poetry* and *Last Poems*. Thomas's Field Notebook from the summer of 1915 shows a common origin for this poem and 'Haymaking': 'Things forgotten – I I have forgotten the names of stars [. . .] ['The Word'] But I remember I Those little copses of blackcaps nettles. bramble where I a man might hide For ever dead or alive. ['Haymaking']' (FNB80, after 2 June 1915, Berg)

HAYMAKING (100): London, 6 or 8 July 1915; *This England*; text: *Poems*.

A DREAM (102): London, '7 & 8' (probably Steep, 8 and 9) July 1915; text: *Last Poems*. Written in the week before he enlisted, Thomas's poem recalls a dream of Frost when 'we were walking near Ledington but we lost one another in a strange place and I woke saying "Somehow someday I shall be here again" which I made the last lines of some verses' (to Frost, 22 July 1915, Dartmouth College).

THE BROOK (103): Steep, 10 July 1915; *An Anthology of New Poetry*; text: *An Anthology of New Poetry* and *Last Poems*. Thomas's Field

Notebook from summer 1915 reveals that the child is 'Baba', his daughter, Myfanwy: '"Nobody's been here before" says Baba paddling in sandy brook – so she thinks,' continuing, 'Mellow the blackbird, tart the thrush' (FNB80, after 2 June 1915, Berg). The poem recalls 'This England' in its struggle to know the value of earth and sun.

ASPENS (104): Steep, 11 July 1915; *Six Poems*; text: *An Anthology of New Poetry* and *Last Poems*. Aspen poplars mark the crossroads at the edge of Steep. Frost thought this 'the loveliest of all' the poems Thomas had written to date (to Thomas, 31 July 1915, Dartmouth College).

THE MILL-WATER (105): Steep, 12 July 1915; text: *Last Poems*. The Ashford Stream falls sixteen feet at Steep Mill.

COCK-CROW (107): London, 23 July 1915; *Six Poems*; text: *Poems*. On 19 July, Thomas had been attested as a private in the Artists Rifles.

A PRIVATE (108): Steep, 6 and 7 January, and 1 August 1915; *Six Poems, An Anthology of New Poetry, Last Poems*; text: *An Anthology of New Poetry*. Two untitled January drafts (of four and six lines respectively) contained no allusion to the war, which was added in August when the poem gained its title and its two final lines, before being sent to Gordon Bottomley for inclusion in *An Anthology of New Poetry*.

THIS IS NO CASE OF PETTY RIGHT OR WRONG (109): Steep, '26 XII 1915'; *Six Poems*; text: *Last Poems*. In September, Thomas went into training camp in High Beech, Essex, before transferring to nearby Hare Hall; he wrote only a handful of poems for the remainder of the year. Though recorded in the Bodleian manuscript as written on Boxing Day, he told Eleanor Farjeon (6 January 1916, Battersea Library) that the poem was begun 'some weeks' before that and completed 7–9 January. The poem reflects Thomas's sustained ambivalence towards the war and his enlistment; the title has no basis in manuscript.

RAIN (110): 'Coming home from Hare Hall', 7 January 1916; text: *Poems*.

THE CLOUDS THAT ARE SO LIGHT (111): Hare Hall, 15 January 1916; text: *Poems*.

ROADS (112): 'Coming home from Hare Hall', 22 January 1916; *An Anthology of New Poetry*; text: *Last Poems*. 'Helen of the roads' is Sarn Helen, one of 'the great old mountain roads' built by the Romans in Wales, said Thomas (to Eleanor Farjeon, 24 January 1916), possibly named after a heroine of the Mabinogion.

FEBRUARY AFTERNOON (115): London, 7 and 8 February 1916; text: *Last Poems*.

I MAY COME NEAR LOVING YOU (116): London, 8 February 1916; text: *Collected Poems* (1949). On New Year's Day 1916, Thomas and his father exacerbated their fractious relationship with a heated argument about the war, which informed the timing of this poem as well as the drafting of 'This is no case of petty right or wrong'. In preparing the 1949 *Collected Poems*, Helen explained, 'The poem was left out of previous editions because the subject of it is Edward's father and it could not be published during his lifetime or Edward's mother's. But there is no reason now to withhold publication and it can be included in the new issue. I wonder if it should have the title "P. H. T." Edward's father's initials' (Helen Thomas to Richard de la Mare [May 1949], Faber Rdlm163). No title is given by Thomas in manuscript or typescript; a first-line title is here preferred to Helen's.

THOSE THINGS THAT POETS SAID (117): London, 9 February 1916; *Last Poems*; text: Bodleian Library. In the winter and spring of 1916, Thomas embarked upon a number of love poems which may have been triggered by his friendship with the painter Edna Clarke Hall. In *Last Poems* and subsequent editions, the first line and title appear as 'These things that poets said', which is a misreading of the only surviving manuscript in the Bodleian Library; Thomas left the poem untitled.

NO ONE SO MUCH AS YOU (118): 'Going home on sick leave', 11 February 1916; text: *Collected Poems* (1928). To protect her feelings, Thomas told Helen that these lines, presumably addressed to a wife or lover, were 'verses to Mother' (24 February 1916), which led to the adoption of the title '[M. E. T.]' in the 1978 edition of the *Collected Poems*. No title appears in either the surviving manuscript or typescript.

THE UNKNOWN (120): Steep, 14 February 1916; *Poetry* (Chicago, February 1917), *An Anthology of New Poetry* and *Last Poems*; text: *An Anthology of New Poetry*.

CELANDINE (122): Hare Hall, 4 March 1916; text: *Last Poems*.

'HOME' (123): Hare Hall, 7 and 10 March 1916; text: *Poems*. Thomas told Frost (5 March, Dartmouth College) he was 'restless' with army camp life in the spring of 1916, and yet ambivalent towards 'home' life in Steep. The inverted commas of the title are Thomas's.

THAW (125): 'Going home', 10 March 1916; text: *Poems*. Letter to Frost, 16 March: 'The weather is changing at last. The snow has melted. The sun is very warm. The rooks in the camp trees are nesting. They wake us at 5.30.'

IF I SHOULD EVER BY CHANCE (126): 'At Little Warley and Hare Hall', 29 March–6 April 1916; *Poems*; text: Bodleian Library. This poem, for the poet's eldest daughter Bronwen, is the first of a quartet of 'household poems' (letter to Gordon Bottomley, 24 April, Cardiff University) written for his family and celebrates the Essex place names nearby Hare Hall. Line 11 is absent from the first draft (notebook M_2, the second that came into Mervyn's possession, 29 March) and does not appear in either *Poems* (the printer's typescript or the publication) or *Collected Poems* (1920). However, the line is written into the fair copy manuscript in the Bodleian (dated 6 April) and is incorporated into the second edition of *Collected Poems* (1928); the pattern of rhyming couplets would indicate that Thomas intended this to be a sonnet, and though he oversaw the preparation of *Poems* the omission of the line from that edition may have been an oversight.

IF I WERE TO OWN (127): Hare Hall, 1–7 April 1916; text: *Poems*. For the poet's son, Mervyn.

WHAT SHALL I GIVE? (129): Hare Hall, 2–8 April 1916; text: *Poems*. For the poet's youngest daughter, Myfanwy.

AND YOU, HELEN (130): Hare Hall, 9 April 1916; text: *Poems*. The last in the quartet of 'household poems', for the poet's wife.

LIKE THE TOUCH OF RAIN (131): Hare Hall, 23–30 April 1916; text: *Poems*. The poem appeared as "'Go now'" in *Collected Poems* (1978), based on a reference in a 1916 letter to Eleanor Farjeon; in fact Thomas chose the first-line title when preparing *Poems*. In his notebook (M_2), the first two stanzas are written in ink and the third in pencil, suggesting that Thomas added the final stanza sometime before producing the fair copy in the Bodleian manuscript on 30 April.

WHEN WE TWO WALKED (132): Hare Hall, 23 April–1 May 1916; text: *Poems*. Drafted on facing pages of his (M_2) notebook on the same day, this poem and 'Like the touch of rain' are the first of two pairs of poems written at this time that formally mirror one another.

TALL NETTLES (133): Hare Hall, 24 April–1 May 1916; text: *Poems*. Thomas made a conscious and formal pairing of this poem with 'The Watchers', drafting them on facing pages of his (M_2) notebook and transcribing them onto the same page when making his fair copy (Bodleian).

THE WATCHERS (134): Hare Hall, 24 April–1 May 1916; *Two Poems* (1927); text: *Collected Poems* (1928). There is no evidence for a title in the notebook, manuscript or typescript in which the poem survives, which must have been adopted by the editor of *Two Poems*.

THE CHERRY TREES (135): [Steep] 7 and 8 May 1916; text: *Poems*. A formal mirror of 'In Memoriam (Easter, 1915)'.

IT RAINS (136): Hare Hall, 11, 12 and 13 May; text: *Poems*. Thomas struggled harder than usual with the first draft of this poem, rewriting the final stanza three times followed by a second full draft in his notebook (M_2) before making his fair copy (Bodleian).

SOME EYES CONDEMN (137): 'Hare Hall and train', 13 and 14 May 1916; text: *Poems*.

THE SUN USED TO SHINE (138): Hare Hall, 22 May 1916; text: *Poems*. The poem recalls the poet's walks in Dymock with Robert Frost in the summer of 1914.

NO ONE CARES LESS THAN I (140): Hare Hall, 25 and 26 May 1916; text: *Last Poems*. In 1915 Thomas had written an appreciation of the late Rupert Brooke, and it seems likely that this poem was written in response to Brooke's 'The Soldier'. Thomas gave no title to the piece in any of his manuscripts; it appeared as '[Bugle Call]' in *Collected Poems* (1978), but the first-line title of *Last Poems* is preferred here.

AS THE TEAM'S HEAD-BRASS (141): Hare Hall, 27 May 1916; text: *Poems*. By the summer of 1916, Thomas was focussed upon leaving his Essex camp for a commission and a posting to France. His working title for the poem was 'The Last Team' (letter to Eleanor Farjeon, 4 June 1916, Battersea).

AFTER YOU SPEAK (143): 'Going home', 3 June 1916; text: *Poems*.

THE GREEN ROADS (144): Hare Hall, 28 June 1916; text: *Poems*. Thomas wrote to Eleanor Farjeon on 29 June, 'The [Epping] forest is a fragment left 6 miles from here, the best of all country. I go there every time I can.' (Battersea)

THE GALLOWS (145): 'Selsfield (with Helen)', 3 and 4 July 1916; text: *Poems*. 'I could not help writing these 4 verses on the theme of some stories I used to tell Baba' (to Eleanor Farjeon, 8 July, Battersea).

GONE, GONE AGAIN (147): Balham and Royal Artillery School, Handel Street, London, 26 or 27 August–3 September 1916; *New Statesman*, 28 April 1917; text: *Poems*. Bodleian manuscript is dated '3 ix 16', but a letter to Eleanor Farjeon of 27 August (Battersea) shows that it existed in draft at an early date: 'I have been resting yesterday and today at Rusham Rd. [. . .] The result is I got tired of logarithms and wrote 8 verses which you see before you.' The poem is retitled 'Blenheim Oranges' in *Collected Poems* (1978) after a reference made by Thomas in a letter (to Farjeon, 19 September 1916, Battersea).

THAT GIRL'S CLEAR EYES (149): Handel Street, 10 September 1916; text: *Last Poems*. The Royal Artillery School at Handel Street was situated near to the Foundlings Hospital, which received its royal charter in 1739. Brunswick Square is the 'stony square sunlit'; the 'dark cloisters' may be the colonnades which still stand around the former perimeter of the hospital (demolished in 1928). The 'airy plane', planted in Victorian times, still dominates the square today. No manuscript evidence for the title.

WHAT WILL THEY DO? (150): 'Going home to Steep', 15 September 1916; text: *Last Poems*. No manuscript evidence for the title.

THE TRUMPET (151): 'Trowbridge Barracks', Royal Artillery, '26–7–8? September 1916'; text: *Poems*. Thomas concealed his poetry from his companions in camp by disguising the verse as prose; he used capital letters to signify line breaks.

WHEN FIRST (152): place and date of composition unknown, possibly 30 September or 1 October 1916; text: *Poems*. No manuscript survives for this poem, only the printer's undated typescript for *Poems*; but two moments in Thomas's personal life suggest themselves as possible triggers for this poem in which the poet walks down Shoulder of Mutton Hill in Steep for 'the last time': his eviction from his study at Wick Green in July 1916 and

Helen's move from Yew Tree Cottage to Essex in October of the same year. 'When first' is one of only two poems missing from a consecutive sequence of sixty-eight in the bound collection of fair copies that now resides in the Bodleian Library. Within that manuscript, a page has been torn out between 'The Trumpet' and 'The Child in the Orchard' (dating the missing page to late September or October 1916); a surviving fragment from the lower left-hand margin of the torn page suggests it contained a draft of twenty-six lines (fewer if it included line or stanza breaks), which feasibly could be a discarded, altered early draft of 'When first' (twenty-four lines, five stanza breaks). Thomas's choice of words may be significant when on 1 October (dated 2 October, Cardiff) he told Gordon Bottomley that he had seen Steep for 'the last time'. However, on 31 December 1916 Thomas told Frost, 'I have rhymed but I have burnt my rhymes and feel proud of it' (Dartmouth College), which, if true, may account for the torn page in the Bodleian manuscript, leaving us none the wiser as to the composition date of the poem.

THE CHILD IN THE ORCHARD (153): High Beech, October 1916; text: *Last Poems*. No manuscript evidence for the title; no typescript survives.

LIGHTS OUT (154): Trowbridge, *c.*1–5 November 1916; text: *Poems*. Thomas's meditation on sleep, with its undercurrent of mortality, 'sums up what I have often thought at that call' (to Eleanor Farjeon, 6 November 1916, Battersea).

THE LONG SMALL ROOM (156): Trowbridge, *c.*1–11 November 1916; text: *Poems*. According to Myfanwy, when Thomas was staying at East Grinstead in the winters of 1912 and 1913 he worked in 'a stone out-building' in the garden grounds of Vivian Locke Ellis's Selsfield House (Myfanwy Thomas, *One of These Fine Days*, Manchester: Carcanet, 1982, 47).

THE LANE (157): Codford, December 1916; *Two Poems*; text: *Collected Poems* (1928). On 22 January 1917, a week before he left for France, Thomas wrote to Helen, 'You never mentioned receiving those verses about Green Lane, Froxfield. Did you get them? They were written in December and suggested by our last walk there in September.' The title was given by the editor of *Two Poems*.

OUT IN THE DARK (158): High Beech, 24 December 1916; text: *Last Poems*. Written over his last Christmas with his family. Thomas told Eleanor Farjeon (27 December, Battersea) that 'it is really Baba who speaks it, not I'. He asked his daughter, 'Did mother tell you I wrote a poem about the dark that evening when you did not want to go into the sitting room because it was dark?' (29 December, Cardiff). Thomas left the poem untitled.

THE SORROW OF TRUE LOVE (168): Lydd, 13 January 1917; *The Anglo-Welsh Review* (1971), *Collected Poems* (1978); text: War Diary. Thomas did not return to this untitled (and probably unfinished) draft, which was written on the inside back cover of the private diary he kept as a soldier in 1917 and given the title 'Last Poem' in *Collected Poems* (1978). On 11 January, he said goodbye to Helen, Mervyn and Myfanwy; on 12 January, to his parents, his brothers, and to his daughter, Bronwen.

Index of Titles and First Lines